Award-winning writer, television broadcaster and author of numerous bestsellers, **Leslie Kenton** is described by the press as 'the guru of health and fitness' and 'the most original voice in health'. A shining example of energy and commitment, she is highly respected for her thorough reporting. Leslie was born in California. She is the daughter of jazz musician Stan Kenton and Violet Peters, a painter. After leaving Stanford University she journeyed to Europe in her early twenties, settling first in Paris then in Britain where she has since remained. She has raised four children on her own by working as a television broadcaster, novelist, writer and teacher on health and for fourteen years she was an editor at *Harpers & Queen.*

Leslie's writing on mainstream health is internationally known and has appeared in *Vogue,* the *Sunday Times, Cosmopolitan* and the *Daily Mail.* She is the author of many other health books including: *the Joy of Beauty, Ultrahealth, Raw Energy* – co-authored with her daughter Susannah – *Ageless Ageing, The Biogenic Diet, Cellulite Revolution, 10 Day Clean-up Plan, Endless Energy, Nature's Child, Lean Revolution* and the *10 Day De-stress Plan.* She turned to fiction with *Ludwig* – her first novel. Former consultant to a medical corporation in the USA and to the Open University's Centre of Continuing Education, Leslie has won several awards for her writing including the PPA 'Technical Writer of the Year'. Her work was honoured by her being asked to deliver the McCarrison Lecture at the Royal Society of Medicine. In recent years she has become increasingly concerned not only with the process of enhancing individual health but also with re-establishing bonds with the earth as a part of helping to heal the planet. Leslie now lives in West Wales in an eighteenth- century house overlooking the sea, once inhabited by Virginia Woolf.

Raw Energy Recipes

From the authors of the bestselling *Raw Energy*

Leslie and Susannah Kenton

EBURY PRESS · LONDON

1 3 5 7 9 10 8 6 4 2

First published in the United Kingdom in 1985
by Century Publishing Co. Ltd

This edition published 1994 by
Ebury Press
Random House
20 Vauxhall Bridge Road
London SW1X 2SA

Random House Australia (Pty) Limited
20 Alfred Street, Milsons Point, Sydney,
New South Wales 2061, Australia

Random House New Zealand Limited
18 Poland Road, Glenfield,
Auckland 10, New Zealand

Random House South Africa (Pty) Limited
PO Box 337, Bergvlei, South Africa

Random House Canada
1265 Aerowood Drive, Mississanga,
Ontario L4W 1B9, Canada

Random House UK Limited Reg. No. 954009

A CIP catalogue record for this book is available from
the British Library

ISBN 0 09 178470 0

Filmset in India by Pure Tech Corporation
Printed and bound in Great Britain
by Clays Ltd, St Ives plc

Papers used by Ebury Press are natural recyclable products
made from wood grown in sustainable forests.

For Joyce Pearce who makes
the best Raw Energy Cuisine
in the Southern Hemisphere

Leslie and Susannah Kenton
Pembrokeshire 1994

Contents

Note

The quantities given in our recipes serve about
four people, unless otherwise stated. We give
approximate measurements as cupfuls
(abbreviated to C – an ordinary cup holds
about 8 fl oz or 225 ml), handfuls,
tablespoons (T) and teaspoons (t).

Introduction

For someone who's never experienced it before there can seem something magical about a high-raw diet. A way of eating in which about 50 to 75 per cent of your foods are taken uncooked increases your vitality, makes you look and feel great, and even helps protect from degenerative illness and premature ageing. Uncooked foods such as fresh crisp vegetables and luscious fruits, natural unprocessed seeds, grains and nuts have a quality of energy which is light yet strong and extraordinarily health-giving. They impart a similar power to the person eating them. Such foods are the richest natural sources of vitamins, minerals and enzymes you will find – all of which are important for high-level health – as well as good-quality protein, easily assimilated complex carbohydrates and essential fatty acids. They are also an excellent source of unadulterated natural fibre.

A high-raw diet has been used in some of Europe's finest clinics for over a hundred years – to cure illness, to increase vitality, to rejuvenate the body, to improve athletic performance, to beautify, and to encourage natural weight loss. It is such a diet that keeps world-famous health spas making money hand over foot as they take in worn, tired, stressed people and transform them in a fortnight into more energetic, younger looking, better functioning versions of themselves. It is a process for which you pay dearly at health farms, clinics and spas, but one which continues to attract those who can afford it because it brings such wonderful results. We've discovered that you can get the same well-proven benefits from a high-raw diet at home right now – *without* paying a fortune – by using the foods readily available in your local shops.

The problem is, suggest to most people that they increase the quantity of uncooked foods in their diet, and they feel quite confused. 'But how?' they ask. 'I can't go on eating salads all the time, can I?' The answer is simple – of course not. *Certainly not*, if you mean by salads the usual limp lettuce leaf with its familiar slice of tomato, cucumber and half a boiled egg. But, as we hope to show you in this book, the range of foods available to create Raw Energy Cuisine is enormous – a real cornucopia of delight. With them you can make beautiful hors d'oeuvres, super soups, salads which are so attractive and delicious they form the centre for a whole meal, plus a myriad of irresistible dressings, luscious drinks, sorbets and ice creams, seductive sweets, rich seed cheeses and dips, as well as breads, loaves and pâtés – a far cry from an ascetic's fare. We use such dishes to create parties which are favourites with children (and good for them too); luxurious slimmer's meals; breakfasts to keep you in top form all day long; dinners which never leave you feeling sluggish or heavy; and what we call our Fabulous Feasts where our massive round table is literally covered with nutritious pleasures for our large family and many friends.

We hope this little book will give you an idea of just how simple, delicious and fun a Raw Energy way of eating can be. In it you will find all the recipes we've used in our Raw Energy television series and video, plus many more which are particular favourites with our family, and some photographs to give you some idea of just how delightful and seductive fresh foods can look. We hope you will try them – and that they will help you gradually increase the number of fresh foods you eat. The recipes should be used far more as guidelines than formulae which are to be strictly followed. Our measurements are not too rigid. One of the many wonderful things about un-cooked foods is that, once you get accustomed to some of the principles of Raw Energy food prep-aration, any recipe is little more than a sugges-tion offering inspiration and encouragement to create your own masterpieces.

When you do we would love to hear about them. Meantime we'd like to share with you some of our best loved recipes. We hope you'll like them!

The Raw Energy Kitchen

The mainstay of our kitchen is not the hob or the oven but our food processor. It is the one piece of equipment we would never want to do without. And because we are such a large family we have one of the big varieties which holds twice the ordinary quantity of soups, vegetables, nuts and sweets. For although most recipes in this book can be made by hand, the addition of a food processor to your kitchen equipment is such a boon in the time and energy it saves (you can prepare a whole salad meal in about five minutes), that it would be a pity to have to do without one – particularly if you are preparing food for more than two people.

A Simple Processor

There are many different models on the market, most of which we have tried, and some of which we have found completely infuriating. Processors vary enormously in their convenience of use as well as their durability. When buying a food processor it is best to choose the simplest one you can find. Those big all-purpose kitchen machines which do everything are not only a pain to put together, take apart and clean, but you are forever hunting for some little part you need for what you are doing when you could have your soup, salad or muesli finished already.

Each machine comes with several attachments. There is a blade which is excellent for grinding nuts and seeds, homogenising vegetables for soups and loaves, and making dressings, dips and sweets. The grater (some come with two – a fine and a coarse) is ideal for fruit when making muesli or for some salads, the slicer for other salads and desserts. Most food processors also have a pastry attachment – a little white plastic blade which we have always found totally useless even for making pastry. The ordinary blade does everything better.

Blender Aid

A blender too can be helpful for making energy shakes or even grinding nuts and seeds – provided you supply yourself with something like a chopstick to clear the blade when you are blending dry ingredients. If you have to choose between a blender and a processor – go for the processor, since you can do everything in it you can do in a blender. But if you are fortunate enough to have both you will probably find that the blender is easier to use for drinks while the processor works better for everything else. Even a coffee grinder can be useful for grinding small quantities of nuts if you have nothing else.

The other piece of equipment which we use often but which is by no means necessary is a centrifuge juicer for extracting vegetables juices and all fruit juices except citrus ones. We love vegetable juices – our favourite is a combination of carrot and apple which we spike with other goodies such as spinach, cabbage, berries, pineapple etc. Once you get used to the taste of fresh apple juice made this way it is like eating real Russian caviar for the first time – you never want the supermarket shelf imitation.

Hand Help

If you don't have access to this kind of electric wizardry – or even if you do – there are some useful little mechanical gadgets which can be enormously useful to the Raw Energy cook. For instance the Swiss, the French and the Dutch have well-designed food mills for grating and chopping which you can use instead of a food processor to shred vegetables and fruits. But when buying one make sure it comes apart easily, has stainless steel blades and is simple to clean. We often use an ordinary stainless steel grater for making single bowls of muesli or for grating cheese. The reason for the stainless steel is that it does not oxidise and therefore does not destroy vitamin C in the foods you are shredding as do many of the other metals.

A Good Edge

Several sharp knives in different sizes and a couple of good chopping boards are indispensable to the Raw Energy chef. Here we break our stainless steel rule simply because you can get a much better edge on a carbon steel knife. A knife sharpener is an absolute must. So is a good vegetable brush – mark it *Vegetables* so it doesn't get used by some uninformed member of the family to scrub the wheels of his car. Another little gadget we use a lot is a salad washer – a basket in which you can spin your washed lettuce leaves to dry them before turning them into a seductive salad.

All together a Raw Energy chef needs very few utensils. You can forget the heavy pots and pans and greasy dishes which are so hard to wash up. Just for the fun of it we tend to collect different salad platters, little dishes for dressings and dips and simple one-person-meal-size bowls for dish salads which we always make sure are made from natural substances – glass, pottery, earthenware or wood rather than plastic or metal. And, of course, we always steer clear of anything made of aluminium that could come in contact with food since in the presence of acid foods such as tomatoes, aluminium oxide tends to form which, when repeatedly taken into the body with the foods, can cause the serious symptoms of aluminium poisoning.

Finally the thing you need most, unless you are going to be cutting your lettuces from the garden one moment and popping them into salads the next, is refrigeration. You can shop a couple of times a week provided you have a good-sized refrigerator to keep fresh things in. We even store our nuts, seeds, and oils in the fridge to protect them from oxidation. And we tend to wash many of our vegetables as soon as we get them home before putting them into vegetable bins in the refrigerator. This means that when we go down to the kitchen to prepare a luscious dish salad for lunch they are all freshly clean and waiting for us. This cuts preparation time down to between three and five minutes per salad.

Breakfasts

Breakfast quite literally means the meal at which you break your fast of the night. It needs to be light but full of the kind of energy that can sustain you through the morning without flagging. Few breakfasts can do that. Eat the standard bowl of processed dried cereal sprinkled with white sugar and you are likely to be reaching for a sticky bun by eleven 'just to see you through'. Go instead for the old- fashioned British breakfast of greasy eggs and bacon, and its high fat content can have you feeling dull-headed while the excess protein tends to make your system acid and you more prone to stress reactions as a result. Raw Energy breakfasts are different. They are fresh, fine-flavoured, sustaining and easy to prepare. They never leave you feeling heavy or over-full.

In this section we include many variations and options because we believe that there is no one 'right' breakfast dish to suit everyone. A manual labourer, for instance, will need a more calorific and sustaining meal than a person who sits behind a desk all day. Also, depending on the season, certain foods are more appropriate and more readily available. So here we suggest recipes for the old and young, for summer and winter. The important thing is to experiment to find which breakfast suits your needs best.

Note about Allergies

Many people, whether they know it or not, suffer from food allergies or sensitivities, the two most common being to milk products and wheat. Such a sensitivity can cause bloatedness, chronic fatigue, abdominal pains, skin blemishes and even depression. Many of our recipes which include either milk products or wheat have milk-free and wheat-free variations for those who prefer to avoid these products. It is sometimes worth eliminating either one or both from your diet for a week or so as an experiment to see if it makes any difference to the way you feel.

Milk is one of the most over-rated foods. It is great for calves but many people feel better without milk or milk products in their diet at all. As for wheat and its most famous ingredient bran – for some it is fine. For others that wonderful wholegrain bread or bran sprinkled on yoghurt or cereals can actually be constipating instead of laxative. There are so many other grains which are excellent sources of fibre. Oats, for example, offer a far more digestible fibre than bran and have health benefits beyond their bulking ability.

Muesli – Swiss Magic

Muesli was originally the invention of the ac-
claimed Swiss physician Max Bircher-Benner who
made it famous as part of his effective system of
healing based on a high-raw diet. It, like the rest
of his nutritional plan, grew out of the discovery
(a discovery which at the time was no less revolu-
tionary than it is today) that when you put sick
people on a diet of all raw or mostly raw foods,
they get better. For this kind of diet appears to
trigger the body's own natural healing powers and
encourage them to re-balance an ailing body, re-
store energy levels and (we have learnt to our
amazement) even help stabilise a troubled mind.
European experts in high-raw nutrition developed
world-wide reputations for their work by curing
thousands of their diverse illnesses – including
the famous Albert Schweitzer of serious diabetes,
and his wife of tuberculosis (a sickness which
early this century was one of our biggest killers).

Muesli was for Bircher-Benner – as it has
become for us – the standard breakfast fare. And,
like his original muesli, our Raw Energy breakfasts bear little resemblance to that heavy sugar-
loaded dry grain variety you can buy in
supermarkets these days. For real muesli is not
centred on grains. It is more a fruit dish with just
a hint of whole grains used as a base. Dried grains
in too great a quantity cause stomach upsets for
many people. But when these grains are used
only in small amounts and when they have been
soaked in a little water overnight their starches

19

break down into natural sugars which are not only sweet but easy to digest. The grains in our muesli give it a sustaining quality which is sufficient for even the most physically active people.

When making muesli you can either use a food processor and do enough for a whole family at once, or with a simple hand grater make one bowl. But be sure to experiment with all the many variations depending on what kind of fruits are in season. Each has its own delicious character.

Raw Muesli

This recipe calls for an apple, but you can use almost any fruit instead, or add extra fruit in season. . . . It serves one person.

2T oatflakes (or a combination of oat, rye, wheat etc.), soaked overnight in a little water or fruit juice (e.g. pineapple), a handful of raisins (soaked), 1 apple or firm pear (grated), 1/2 lemon, 2T plain yoghurt, 1t honey, 1T chopped nuts (e.g. almonds and Brazils), 1/2t powdered cinnamon or ginger

Mix together the soaked oatflakes and the raisins. Combine with this mixture a grated apple or pear with a squeeze of lemon juice and the natural plain yoghurt. Drizzle with honey and sprinkle with chopped nuts and cinnamon or ginger.

Banana Muesli Add a banana sliced in quarters lengthwise and then chopped crosswise into small pieces. Or mash a banana with a little yoghurt or fruit juice and use as a topping.

Summer Muesli Add a handful of raspberries, strawberries, blackcurrants or pitted cherries to the basic muesli, or substitute the apple for a finely diced peach or nectarine.

Winter Muesli Soak a selection of dried fruits – such as apricots, sultanas, figs, dates, pears – overnight in water. Dice into small pieces, or cut up with a pair of scissors and add to the other muesli ingredients. Spice with a pinch of nutmeg.

Dairy-Free Muesli Substitute the yoghurt for some fresh fruit juice such as apple, orange or grape. To thicken the juice, blend with a little fresh fruit such as banana, pear or apple.

Blended Muesli For old people or young children it is a good idea to blend all the muesli ingredients together in a processor. This gives a nourishing and delicious purée which requires no chewing.

Fruit

Not only are fruits some of the most delicious natural foods available, they also have remarkable properties for spring-cleaning the body and are excellent biochemical antidotes to stress.

Because fruits contain many natural acids such as citric and malic acid, they have an acid pH reaction in digestion; however, since they are also a rich source of alkaline-forming minerals, their reaction in the blood is alkaline. This reaction helps neutralise the acidic by-products of stress as well as the waste products of metabolism which are also acidic. That is why fruits are so highly prized as a means of internally cleansing the body. Many healthy people insist that a few days on fruit alone helps clear out whatever internal rubbish they need to get rid of, and leaves them looking and feeling great.

Fruit contains very little protein but it is very high in the mineral potassium which needs to be balanced with sodium for perfect health in the body. Because most people in the West eat far too much sodium in the form of table salt and an excess of protein as well (which leaches important minerals from the bones and tissues), eating good quantities of fruit can help re-balance a body, improve its functioning, and make you feel more energetic as well. Fruit also contains natural sugars together with natural fibre. This combination means that your body is able to make good use of the energy such natural sugars provide without experiencing blood-sugar problems which lead to fatigue and can come from eating refined sugar. Fruit is also an important source of certain vitamins and minerals which are particularly important in protecting you from illness – especially vitamin C.

Finally, because fruits are naturally sweet and because we are born with an innate liking for sweet things, a snack of fruit or a sweet of fresh fruit after a meal can be tremendously satisfying to the palate. And there is such a variety of beautiful textures, colours and tastes to choose from – from the sensuous softness of persimmons and the super-sweetness of fresh figs, to the exhilarating crunch of the finest English apple.

Some Delicious and Nutritious Muesli Sprinkles

These are 'extras' which can be placed in bowls at the breakfast table for people to help themselves to.

THREE-SEED MIX Grind together in a blender or processor 1C each of sesame, sunflower and pumpkin seeds. (Grind the sesame seeds first on their own very well until their husks are broken down, then add the other seeds and blend.) Keep the mixture in an airtight jar in the fridge and use to sprinkle on mueslis or salads. The three seeds together make an excellent complement of protein and essential fatty acids.

COCONUT One of our favourite sprinkles is dried coconut flakes toasted lightly under the grill until golden brown. You can mix the coconut with sesame seeds and toast together for a tasty and nutritious sprinkle.

WHEATGERM This, too, is delicious toasted. Sprinkle a tablespoon over a bowl of muesli for added vitamins B and E.

MOLASSES If you can find unsulphured molasses it makes a wonderful vitamin-and mineral-rich sweetener to replace honey for muesli. But beware of sulphured molasses – it tastes revolting!

NUTS A few toasted whole nuts such as hazels make a nice crunchy addition to a creamy muesli.

LECITHIN Especially good for slimmers, a little lecithin sprinkled into a bowl of muesli may help emulsify the fats in the body and provides several important nutrients. For Slimmer's Porridge, see page 74.

Energy Shakes

One of our favourite breakfasts is a Raw Energy shake. You simply put all the ingredients you want into a blender or food processor and whip them up in seconds to give a sustaining instant drink. One of us, Susannah, does a lot of dancing and running, and finds that an energy shake, which is easy to digest and packed with goodness, is the ideal breakfast for instant and sustained energy.

Yoghurt Shake
1C plain yoghurt, 1 ripe banana, few drops vanilla essence, 1t honey, 1t coconut (optional)

Combine the ingredients thoroughly in a blender. As a variation try replacing the banana with a handful of berries, half a papaya or mango, or a few chunks of fresh pineapple.

Nut-Milk Shake
This is the dairy-free alternative to the first shake. For extra goodness add a teaspoon of brewer's yeast (the de-bittered kind is the most bearable), a tablespoon of wheatgerm, or the yolk of an egg, and blend well.

$^1/_3$ C almonds (blanched), $^2/_3$ C water, 5 pitted dates, few drops vanilla essence, 1t honey

Blend the almonds and the water really well until the mixture is smooth. You can use un-blanched almonds and strain the mixture at this point to remove the ground-up husks. Add the other ingredients and process well. Serve imme-diately.

Apricot Shake Use apricots, fresh or dried, in-stead of the dates and add a handful of sunflower seeds to the nuts before you blend.

Grape Shake Use fruit juice such as grape (or apple) instead of the water, and raisins in-stead of the dates. Omit the honey and vanilla if desired.

You can make the yoghurt drink with milk for a thinner beverage – soya milk is nice.

If you are using yoghurt, why not try making your own? It's very simple and doesn't require a lot of expensive equipment. The easiest way to make it is in a wide-mouthed flask, but an earth-enware crock or dish kept in a warm place will do just as well. We use two methods – the traditional one where you warm your milk to blood heat, and a simplified method that calls for warm water and powdered skimmed milk.

Home-Made Yoghurt
We prefer goat's milk to cow's because it is richer in vitamins and minerals, and because its fats are emulsified which makes it easier to digest. In fact, many people who are allergic to cow's milk can take goat's or sheep's milk quite com-fortably.

*2 pints (about a litre) milk (preferably goat's or sheep's),
2 heaped tablespoons plain natural yoghurt (starter)*

Warm milk in a saucepan to just above blood heat (test it as you would a baby's bottle). Pour into a flask or crock and add 2 heaped tablespoons of plain natural yoghurt. This can be cow's or goat's yoghurt, but it is important that it is *live yoghurt*, and that it doesn't have any fruit or sugar in it. Read the label to be sure that it contains a real yoghurt culture which is needed to transform the milk.

Stir the starter in well and replace the lid of the thermos flask. If you are using a non-insulated container, wrap it in a blanket and place it in an airing cupboard or on top of a radiator. If you have an Aga or Rayburn, place the dish on a wire cooling tray on top of it. Otherwise you can heat an oven for ten minutes as hot as it can go and then switch it off. Put the container inside and leave it, without opening the door, overnight. After 6–8 hours you will have cultured the yoghurt.

Transfer it to the fridge and use it for muesli, drinks, soups, dressings, frozen desserts etc. You can then use this yoghurt as the starter for your next batch and go on indefinitely. If your yoghurt goes sour, you'll have to buy another starter and begin afresh.

Instant Low-Fat Yoghurt
One of the very simplest methods for making yoghurt is to use low-fat skimmed milk powder.

Make up two pints (about a litre) of milk in a blender, using one and a half times the amount of powdered milk suggested on the packet. If you use boiling water from a kettle and add cold water to it you can get just the temperature of milk you need and don't have to bother heating your milk in a saucepan. Add the two tablespoons of plain yoghurt as in the ordinary method and leave in a suitable container for about eight hours. If you want a really thick yoghurt, e.g. for dips, simply add more skimmed milk powder when you make up the milk.

Coffee

For many people the focus of breakfast is a cup of coffee – or several. They rely on coffee to give them the pick-me-up they need to get themselves off to work. The problem with coffee is that its stimulating benefits are short-lived, so that by the time eleven o'clock comes around you find you need another cup to keep you going and by the end of the day you have consumed half a dozen cupfuls and still feel exhausted. For this reason the Raw Energy breakfast eliminates coffee altogether. The kinds of fresh energy-rich foods contained in our mueslis and shakes will give you the *sustained* energy you need.

Coffee also robs your body of many valuable minerals necessary for optimal health. If you like a warm drink it is far better to try one of the cereal beverages made of chicory and barley sweetened with a little honey or molasses. Or try a herb tea blend – see the section on herb teas on page 83 for suggestions.

Lunches

The ideal Raw Energy lunch is a splendid dish salad filled with different vegetables, fruits, sprouted seeds, dips and seed and nut cheeses. We prepare one of these salads for each member of the family in large individual dishes in a matter of minutes. And because each person has his own salad, if there is one particular vegetable he doesn't like – onions, say – it can be left out very easily.

Each time we make a dish salad the ingredients vary depending on what we have available. We are always experimenting with new ways of chopping and combining vegetables, fruits etc. We also grow our own sprouted seeds and beans and then keep them in the fridge in polythene bags to sprinkle over salads. Seed and nut cheeses make a delicious but rich contribution to such a salad. We sometimes spoon a little straight into the dish salad or spread some onto pumpernickel bread, rye crackers or oatcakes to eat with it. The dressings we use for dish salads are what we call dip-dressings. They are thick dressings which can be used as dips to dunk crudités into, or thinned a little with water or juice to pour over vegetables. Finally we often toast a few seeds – pumpkin, sunflower or sesame – to sprinkle over the top of the salad.

Dish salads vary from the elaborate to the very simple: for example a selection of fresh greens – lettuces and herbs straight from the garden – torn into bite-sized pieces, tossed with a handful of chopped spring onions and topped with a tofu or hummus dressing. Here are a few examples to give the general idea. After that it's up to you to improvise and make up your own combinations with whatever you like best. (As you'll see, we deliberately haven't specified quantities.)

Dish Salad 1

Make a base of radicchio leaves (or any other lettuce) to line the dish. Then arrange in segments:

> grated carrot placed inside a ring of red pepper and topped with a few fresh garden peas
> a small bunch of watercress inside a ring of sweet yellow pepper
> half an avocado (brush with lemon juice or olive oil to prevent it going brown) filled with radish slices
> a handful of Chinese bean sprouts (mung)
> a few diagonal slices of cucumber
> a few cauliflower and broccoli florets
> some grated raw beetroot
> some grated white radish
> mustard and cress

a tomato sliced into segments – but not all the way through – so that it looks like flower petals.

Dish Salad 2

Line bowl with chopped Chinese leaves, then arrange the following:

celery and carrot sticks looped through rings of sweet peppers

a few slices of fennel

a few slices of baby turnip (raw)

some mangetout (topped and tailed)

some slices of apple

slices of red onion

radish roses (made by cutting zig-zags around the middle of the radish and separating two halves)

a small bunch of grapes

watercress and parsley

an orange sliced in segments with the skin left on for decoration, but peeled back in sections so that it can easily be removed

a handful of chickpea sprouts

Dish Salad 3

Make a base with alfalfa sprouts, then:

arrange around the dish grated carrot, red cabbage, white cabbage and beetroot

add sliced mushrooms, black olives and spring onions

sprinkle raisins over the grated vegetables and add a spoonful of seed and nut cheese (see page 37)

Dish Salad 4

Make a base by shredding tender spinach leaves
finely (remove the stalks), then arrange around
the dish:

a handful of baby button mushrooms with their
stems trimmed
half an avocado, diced (simply slice the flesh in
its shell several times first vertically and then
horizontally, then scoop out the avocado with
a spoon)
some diced red pepper
apple rings (remove the core from the apple
and slice crosswise)
thin slices of Jerusalem artichoke, kohlrabi or
new potatoes (raw)
toasted pumpkin seeds

Dish Salad 5

Use shredded iceberg lettuce as a base, then arrange:

thin slices of carrot and courgette (the slicer attachment on a food processor is ideal for this)
a few cherry tomatoes
sweetcorn (raw, scraped off the cob, or cooked
on the cob)
a few toasted hazelnuts
mustard and cress

The appearance of a dish salad is very important. Fortunately the brilliant colours of fresh
vegetables and fruits are quite stunning. It is nice
to experiment with different decorative ways of

(*Above*) Energy shakes – banana, apricot and grape – are ideal for athletes

(*Overleaf*) Raw Energy Muesli and the three seeds – pumpkin, sunflower and sesame – with herb tea for breakfast

(*Right*) A Raw Energy dish salad lunch

Sprouts, the wonder foods – grow your own for vitamins,
value and vitality

chopping fruits and vegetables to make attractive garnishes.

Dip-Dressings

Here are some of our favourite dip-dressings. We particularly like them with dish salads because of their lovely textures, but of course you can use a regular vinaigrette or mayonnaise-type dressing instead. (For more dressing suggestions see pages 51–55)

Curried Avocado
Even those who say they don't like avocados adore this one!

1–2 avocados, 1C (more or less, to give the desired consistency) fresh orange juice, 1t curry powder, 2t vegetable bouillon powder, fresh herbs (e.g. lovage and French parsley), 1 small clove garlic (optional)

Peel and stone the avocado(s). Blend all the ingredients together in a food processor until smooth.

Raw Hummus
1C chickpea sprouts (about 1 inch or 2 cm long), juice of 1 lemon, a little orange juice to thin, 1 clove garlic, vegetable bouillon powder, 2T tahini, chives or spring onions, paprika

Blend the chickpea sprouts very finely in the food processor. Add lemon and orange juices, garlic, bouillon powder and tahini, and blend well. Spoon into a bowl and top with chopped chives or spring onions, and paprika.

Tofu Dip

1C tofu, juice of 1 lemon, 1t wholegrain Meaux mustard, vegetable bouillon powder, fresh basil and mint

Combine all the ingredients well in the food processor.

Creamed Carrot

1–2 carrots (roughly chopped), 1C tofu or cream/cottage cheese, ¼C walnuts, a handful of fresh parsley, pinch nutmeg, vegetable bouillon powder, a little water or carrot juice to thin, a few slivers of carrot to garnish

Blend the carrots well in the processor along with the tofu or cheese and nuts. Add the herbs and seasonings and a little water or juice to thin if desired. Serve in a bowl sprinkled with carrot slivers.

Ginger Dressing

1C tofu, juice of 1 lemon, 1t grated lemon rind, 1t honey, 1t freshly grated ginger root, 1 clove garlic (pressed), 1T red wine

Blend all the ingredients together well in the food processor.

Yoghurt-Cucumber

½ cucumber, 1C thick yoghurt, 1T vinegar, 1t honey, 1t crushed dill and coriander, handful of walnuts, vegetable bouillon powder, garlic (optional), fresh mint

Peel the cucumber (the skin tends to make the dressing bitter) and chop roughly. Put in the processor with the other ingredients (except mint) and blend well. Serve chilled decorated with mint sprigs.

Dracula's Delight

1 small beetroot, 1C toasted or raw sunflower seeds, 2 lemons, 2T tamari, cayenne, thyme, vegetable bouillon powder, a little water to give desired consistency

Scrub and grate the beetroot. Combine in the processor with the other ingredients plus 1t grated lemon rind. Blend well and adjust the seasoning to taste.

Tomato Treat

4–5 large tomatoes, $1/_2$ C almonds, 1T tahini, juice of 1 lemon, 2 spring onions (chopped), handful of fresh basil leaves, tarragon, freshly ground black pepper, vegetable bouillon powder

Blanch the tomatoes by dropping them in boiling water for a few moments, then remove skins. Grind the almonds in the food processor and add the tomatoes and other ingredients. Save a few spring onion bits to sprinkle over the top of the dressing. Blend the mixture thoroughly and thin with a little water if necessary.

Creamy Mushroom

$1/_4$ C cashew nuts, 1C mushrooms (washed and trimmed), $1/_4$ C water, 1T minced onion, 1t Meaux mustard, 1t tamari, ground black pepper, parsley

Grind the nuts first in the food processor. Then add all the other ingredients (except parsley) and blend thoroughly. Garnish with fresh parsley.

Island Dip
1C egg mayonnaise (see page 52), 1T Whole Earth Tomato Ketchup, 1t Meaux mustard, 2 hard-boiled eggs, a few olives, slices of red pepper or raw beetroot, fresh parsley

Combine the mayonnaise, ketchup and mustard. Chop the eggs finely – the small grater attachment on a food processor is ideal. Pit and chop the olives and finely chop the red pepper or beetroot, and parsley. Combine all the ingredients well and thin with a little water if necessary.

Seed and Nut Cheeses

These are called cheeses because, just like dairy cheeses, they undergo the process of fermentation where some of the protein they contain is partially digested by bacteria. These cheeses are made from ground seeds and nuts. The basic recipe is very simple. Once you have made the cheese base you can add whatever seasoning and spices you wish. You then let it sit for about eight hours (or overnight) in a warm place to ferment. You can also eat seed cheeses freshly made if you prefer.

Basic Seed and Nut Cheese

1C nuts (e.g. cashews, almonds, pecans), 1C seeds (sunflower, pumpkin), $3/4–1C$ water, 1t vegetable bouillon powder

Blend the nuts and seeds finely in a food processor. Add the water and bouillon powder and blend to give a firm paste. (At this point we usually divide the mixture into two parts and season each differently. Choose seasonings from the list below) Combine bases well with the seasonings. Turn into dishes. Leave covered with a tea towel for several hours. Refrigerate and use to spread on vegetable and fruit slices – e.g. apples, cucumbers, carrots, lettuce leaves – or spread thinly on crackers.

Sage and Onion Add 2 spring onions or a little minced red onion, 6 sage leaves (or 1t dried) and 2T wine to the basic recipe and garnish with a little chopped onion.

Garlic and Herb Add 2T mixed fresh (or 2t dried) herbs – e.g. parsley and oregano – 1 clove garlic and juice of $1/2$ lemon.

Nutmeg Add $1/2$ t freshly ground nutmeg and 1t tahini.

Curry Add 1t curry powder and a squeeze of lemon juice.

Caraway Add 2t toasted seeds to the base.

We often eat oatcakes or rye crackers with lunch and have a glass of vegetable or fruit juice or mineral water. Sometimes we like to eat our own home-made crackers which are raw and have to be made ahead of time to dry and crisp up.

One of our favourites is Sunflower Wafers which can be made savoury or sweet and make great snacks at any time during the day.

Savoury Sunflower Wafers
2T sesame seeds (toasted if you prefer), 1C sunflower seeds, 1T tamari, 2T water, few chopped chives

Grind the sesame seeds finely in the food processor. Add the remaining ingredients and grind well. The mixture should be of a stiff dough consistency. Pinch off small pieces and roll into balls. Flatten down on a board with the palm of your hand and then use a fish slice to lift off. Place on a wire cooling tray and leave in a warm place or in the sun to dry out.

Sweet Sunflower Wafers
Follow the same instructions as above but using the following as ingredients.

1C sunflower seeds, ¼C raisins or sultanas, ½t cinnamon or allspice, 2T water

Supersalads

A Supersalad is the focus of the main meal of the day whether it be lunch or dinner. The salad is given the position of honour and the meat, fish, chicken, game, eggs or grain assume the normal position of the 'side salad'. In this way 50 to 75 per cent of the meal is raw. The 'side' dishes can be served in a separate bowl next to the salad or combined with the salad. For example, we often toss chopped hard-boiled egg into a salad, lay slivers of roasted chicken breast on top of a salad or make a vegetable salad with a base of cold cooked rice, millet or buckwheat. Then there are the dressings which range from egg and tahini mayonnaises to French and seed and nut dressings. To finish off the Supersalad we prepare a range of delicious salad sprinkles to dredge over the top.

In this section you will find major and minor salads. The major salads are substantial meals in themselves. The minor salads can be served with other dishes, for example with fish, poultry or game, lentil stews or grain dishes such as brown rice, or several of them can be made and served together as separate courses to make up a main meal. Either way you'll find salad recipes for all year round as well as some unusual and exciting taste combinations.

Major Salads

Garden Crunch

We like to use purple sprouting broccoli from the garden in this, but the ordinary green variety, or a mixture of both, is just as good.

½ iceberg lettuce, 2 or 3 broccoli stalks (use the stems as well as the tops), 1C finely shredded red cabbage, 2–3 tomatoes, several mushrooms, handful of fresh garden peas, 1 shallot or small red onion, a handful of toasted pumpkin seeds

Shred the lettuce and place in a bowl. Add the broccoli tops broken into small pieces, and the stems peeled and sliced crosswise. Shred the red cabbage really finely, chop the tomatoes and slice the mushrooms. Add the peas and the shallot or onion cut into rings. Toss all the ingredients together and top with toasted pumpkin seeds. Serve with a thinned mayonnaise dressing.

Summer Symphony

This salad is a play of colours and shapes – the more variety, and the more you grow yourself, the better.

1 small head of lettuce (Cos is good), 1C small cauliflower florets, 2 celery stalks (finely chopped first lengthwise, then crosswise), 2 carrots (coarsely grated or cut into matchsticks), 6 whole cherry tomatoes, 4 sliced radishes, 1 green pepper cut into thin strips, a few leaves of watercress, sweetcorn off the cob or alfalfa sprouts to garnish

Place the lettuce leaves, torn into bite-sized pieces or shredded, into a bowl – a clear glass bowl is nice for this one as you can see all the beautiful colours through it. Prepare the vegetables and arrange in layers in the bowl. Dress with a thinned mayonnaise dressing, perhaps blended with a tomato or two, and top with sweetcorn or alfalfa sprouts. You can lay slivers of chicken breast on the top as in the picture, and sprinkle with paprika.

Spun Spinach Salad

Many people grow spinach in their gardens and don't know what to do with it. This salad really makes the most of it. You can use any greens instead of spinach, such as perpetual beet or even lettuce. Try to choose the young leaves as they are more tender and sweet. Save the older ones for cooking.

A large bunch of spinach leaves (stems removed), 3 spring onions, 2 handfuls of button mushrooms (finely sliced), a few red radishes (sliced), a handful of toasted cashews or sunflower seeds, 3 hard-boiled eggs

The trick here is to make the spinach look spun. Use a very sharp knife and hold the bunched together leaves tightly in one hand. Cut them as finely as possible as if you were cutting wafer-thin slices of bread. The result will be long thin green strips which look and taste delicious. Chop the spring onions finely so that their taste blends with the spinach and add the other ingredients. The mushrooms should be sliced crosswise – leaving the stems on and just trimming the ends if they look tatty. Peel the hard-boiled eggs and chop or grate into the salad. Toss with a French dressing with garlic.

Italian Salad

The Italians make some of the most delicious salads of all because they grow such splendid vegetables. When we visit Italy we buy several packets of seeds to grow different types of lettuces and basil in our own garden.

1 Italian red lettuce (radicchio) and 1 small Cos lettuce (both finely shredded), 1 red and 1 yellow sweet pepper cut into rings, 1–2 large Italian tomatoes (sliced), 4 radishes (cut into segments), 1 red onion (cut into thin rings), a few thinly sliced button mushrooms, fennel seeds, sliced Mozzarella cheese (optional)

Make a nest of the two shredded lettuces in a shallow dish and arrange the other vegetables in the centre, sprinkling the onion and mushroom slices in last. Toss with a spicy Italian dressing with lots of fresh basil, and sprinkle with toasted fennel seeds, sliced cheese, and freshly ground black pepper if desired.

Jungle Slaw

2C white cabbage (shredded or finely grated), a handful of tender green beans (raw or steamed, cut into slivers diagonally), 2 carrots (grated), ¹/₂ onion (grated), ¹/₂ red or yellow pepper (chopped into very small pieces), 1C unsalted peanuts (toasted under the grill until golden)

Combine all the ingredients except the peanuts. Make a dressing with peanut oil (if possible) and orange juice (see Citrus French dressing for a guideline, page 59). You can add a little chopped chilli pepper if you're adventurous. Add the peanuts at the last minute so that they don't become soggy.

Sunshine Salad

We often add fresh or dried fruits to savoury salads for a delightful flavour contrast. Fresh pineapple is wonderful. It contains as enzyme, bromelain, which helps digest protein. Make sure it is ripe by pulling out one of its centre leaves. If it comes out quite easily, then it is ready to use.

A few leaves of crisp lettuce, 1 medium-sized fresh pineapple, 2 coarsely grated carrots, 2 finely chopped sticks of celery, 2 handfuls of sultanas (or raisins) soaked in water for a few hours to plump them up if possible, ¹/₂t celery seeds, 1t dry mustard mixed with mayonnaise for dressing, wheat sprout roasts (see Sprinkles, page 50).

Wash then crisp the lettuce leaves in the fridge. Peel the pineapple – it isn't necessary to core it – and dice it into fairly small cubes. Prepare the carrots and celery. Combine these with the

43

pineapple and add the sultanas. Sprinkle with celery seeds and serve on the bed of crisp lettuce leaves with a light mayonnaise or French dressing. Sprinkle finally with wheat sprout roasts.

High-Fibre Salad
This salad is made with a base of rice, millet or buckwheat which has been cooked and then cooled. The grains make a filling salad while supplying plenty of good-quality fibre.

2 sticks celery, 1 carrot, 2 tomatoes, ½ red pepper, 3C cooked brown rice, millet or buckwheat, handful of walnuts, 2 spring onions

Finely dice the celery, carrot, tomatoes and red pepper. Stir into the grain with a handful of walnuts. Top with chopped spring onions and dress with a French dressing with lots of fresh parsley.

Vegetables

Fresh raw vegetables are surely the most neglected of all foods for health. Our consumption of these live foods has decreased dramatically in the last fifty years as a result of sophisticated food processing and changes in dietary habits. When grown on healthy soil and carefully prepared, these humble yet beautiful products of the earth are not only irresistibly delicious, they are also potent protectors against premature ageing and the degenerative illnesses which plague Western civilisation in the twentieth century. In clinical studies and laboratory experiments raw vegetables and fruits have been shown to protect against cancer in animals, to lower cholesterol levels in the blood, and to increase stamina and endurance.

Many people avoid fresh vegetables believing that they are not really the important foods because they don't contain protein – so they fill themselves with cooked foods, meat, eggs and milk products instead. In fact cooking changes the biochemical structure of amino acids – the building blocks of proteins – and fatty acids, and makes them only partly digestible. At the world-famous Max Planck Institute for Nutritional Research in Germany, scientists have shown that you need only half the amount of protein in your diet if you eat protein foods raw instead of cooked. Some green vegetables contain proteins of the highest quality. Eaten together with whole-grain bread and legumes or pulses they provide the best quality protein you will find anywhere without the added fat you get from meat. For instance a green salad has a very high protein value in proportion to its calories. And vegetable protein has another important advantage as well: unlike meat or milk products, it does not come with lots of fat attached. Finally, fresh raw vegetables are high in natural unadulterated fibre.

The best vegetables are those you grow yourself organically. If you are lucky enough to have a garden – even a small one – save all the uncooked leftovers and turn them into compost for fertiliser. Even in winter you can grow some

delicious salads and root vegetables in a green-
house or under cloches. The quality of organic
produce is far superior to chemically fertilised
fruits and vegetables – not to mention all of the
vitamins which are lost in foods when they are
picked, stored, shipped and sit on shop shelves.
We go to the garden to pick our vegetables and
fifteen minutes later they are gracing our dinner
table in salad bowls. That is the best way to
preserve their nutritional value as well as to experience the fullness of their flavour. If you are a
flat dweller without a garden you can sprout fresh
seeds and grains in jars or trays on your window-
sill (see page 64).

How you treat your vegetables once you cut
them or buy them from the shops also deter-
mines a lot how they taste, and how much of their
energy-enhancing goodness you preserve. Scrub
anything that will stand up to a good scrubbing,
using a brush marked *Veg Only*. Scrubbing vegetables is better than peeling since many of the
valuable vitamins and minerals are stored direct-
ly beneath their skins. Never soak vegetables for
long periods. They are better washed briefly
under running water so you don't allow water-
soluble vitamins to leach out of them. Always keep
vegetables as cool as possible (even carrots and
turnips are best kept in the refrigerator), and use
them as soon as you can. When shopping for
fresh things be demanding – choose your own
cauliflower and make sure it is a good one. Don't
be intimidated by pushy greengrocers who want
to pass off on to you the leftovers before they

bring their new stock in. Demand the best and you will get it. Your palate and your health will be grateful that you do.

Minor Salads

These are some of the very simple lighter salads. You can serve several together as a full meal or use one instead of having cooked vegetables with your meat, fish etc.

Wild Gypsy Salad

Most people groan at the thought of a green salad – envisaging wilted rubbery lettuce leaves with a piece of floppy cucumber. For us green salad is one of the greatest raw food delights. We grow all sorts of lettuces and greens in our garden and toss them together with our favourite herbs to make this simple but seductive salad.

There is no precise recipe for it, as each time we make it it turns out a little different.

Gather a few of the following: Cos lettuce, butterhead, sugarloaf, radicchio, iceberg, curly endive, dandelion leaves, sorrel, chard, purslane, chickweed, lamb's lettuce, corn salad, land and garden cress, mustard and cress, salad rape, tarragon, parsley, nasturtium, chervil, basil, lovage, lemon balm and marjoram

Rinse the leaves and herbs and spin dry. Place in a tied polythene bag in the fridge for a few minutes to crisp up. Tear the leaves into bite-sized pieces and toss into a bowl. Add some finely chopped chives or spring onions if desired. You can also add a couple of tablespoons of toasted sesame seeds or some sliced radishes. (See Salad Sprinkles page 50, for more ideas.) Dress with a citrus or mustardy French dressing and serve at once.

Winter Chunk Salad

Slaws are ideal winter salads because in the cold months when lettuce is hard to come by cabbage is a staple. Another perfect ingredient for the winter season is sprouted seeds and beans which can be grown anytime anywhere (see sprouting instructions, pages 62–67). To make this salad you simply combine whatever winter vegetables and sprouts you have available and toss them together with a creamy mayonnaise dressing.

Select three of the following and grate: carrots, turnip, Jerusalem artichokes, kohlrabi, white radish, beetroot. Add a handful of mixed sprouts – e.g. mung, lentil, wheat, alfalfa, fenugreek or chick-pea. Combine with a handful of raisins and toss with a mayonnaise dressing spiced with nutmeg.

Avocado Citrus Salad

2–3 avocados, 2 oranges (or 1 grapefruit or 3 satsumas), curly endive, watercress, alfalfa sprouts, paprika

Peel and stone the avocados. Cut in slices length-wise. Peel and slice the citrus fruit and halve the slices. Make a bed of curly endive on a large plate and lay alternating slices of avocado and citrus fruit on it. Garnish with watercress and alfalfa and dust with paprika. Serve with a citrus French dressing (see p. 59).

Crisp Carrot Salad
6–8 fresh carrots, 3 spring onions, mustard and cress,
juice of 1 lemon and 1 orange, 1t wholegrain mustard,
2t honey, ¹/₂t vegetable bouillon powder, 3T olive oil,
1T fresh chopped parsley, freshly ground black pepper

Scrub the carrots well and top and tail. Slice very finely crosswise, if possible with the slicer attachment of a food processor. Finely chop the spring onions and add to the carrots along with the mustard and cress. Combine the remaining ingredients and pour over the salad. Toss well.

Bulgar Salad
3C wheat sprouts, 3 tomatoes, 2 spring onions, hand-
ful of black olives, alfalfa sprouts, parsley and mint

Lay the wheat sprouts in a flat dish. Slice the tomatoes and spring onions and place in a layer on top of the wheat. Add the olives and sprinkle with alfalfa sprouts, fresh parsley and mint. Serve with a lemon and olive oil dressing.

Apple Ginger Salad
Another very simple salad that goes with almost any dish. The ginger is a natural digest-aid.

6 green apples (Granny Smith's are best), ¹/₄C fresh
orange juice, 1t fresh grated ginger, 2t clear honey,
3T toasted sesame seeds

Quarter the apples, remove the cores and then finely slice by hand or in a processor. Combine the orange juice, ginger and honey, and pour over the apples immediately to prevent them going brown. Add the toasted sesame seeds and toss well.

Sprinkles

Whatever your salad, whether a full mixed salad or a simple lettuce salad, it can almost certainly be improved by salad sprinkles. These can be put on to the top of the salad or placed on the table in small dishes for people to help themselves.

THE THREE SEEDS
Any or all of them – sunflower, pumpkin and sesame – straight, ground or toasted.

OTHER SEEDS
Fennel, celery, poppy, caraway, dill, cumin (plain or toasted).

MUSTARD AND CRESS

MINCED NUTS

FRESH HERBS
Parsley, basil, marjoram, mint, fennel, lovage, thyme, tarragon, savory, lemon balm.

SPROUTED SEEDS AND PULSES
See page 64.

SEAWEED
Nori – a type of seaweed which is dried and pressed into thin sheets. Delicious toasted and crumbled on to a salad.

FLOWER PETALS
Such as marigolds, nasturtiums, roses.

SOYA NUTS
These are wonderful! You simply bake soya sprouts (sprinkled with garlic powder or veget-

able bouillon powder) in a moderate oven for about 15 minutes, or until brown and crunchy.

WHEAT AND BARLEY ROASTS

These have a lovely sweet flavour. Bake wheat and/or barley sprouts on a baking sheet as for soya nuts.

HARD-BOILED EGGS

Particularly attractive if you separate the yolk and white once boiled, and grate, then sprinkle in strips of white and yellow over a salad.

CHICKPEAS

Cooked and cooled then tossed into a slaw or leafy salad.

ARTICHOKE HEARTS

One exception to the 'no tinned food' general rule because they are *so* delicious.

FINELY GRATED BEETROOT

Adds colour to bland-looking salads.

GRATED HARD CHEESE
TOFU SLICES
SLICES OR STRIPS OF COLD BAKED POTATO
COLOURED POWDERS

Paprika, cayenne and cumin are nice dusted over pale vegetables and dressings to brighten them up.

Super Dressings

Far too many people tend to rely on bottled salad-cream type dressings which are not only full of chemical additives, sugar and saturated fats, but which completely obliterate all the subtle flavours of a good salad. We always make our own salad dressings, whether they be vinaigrettes or mayonnaises, and keep them in airtight jars in the fridge to use over several days. That way you can be sure to use the best, freshest oils and you can experiment with wonderful herbs and spices to get a range of different flavours. In this section there are three main types of dressings: mayonnaises (egg and tahini based), oil/French, and seed/nut dressings. Try making one salad and dressing it two ways – you'll be surprised at what variety you can get by simply changing the dressing.

Egg Mayonnaises

Mayonnaises are best for coleslaws, sprout, and finely chopped mixed vegetable salads. They are thick and creamy and so give body to a salad. Alternatively they can be diluted with a little water and served over a leafy salad.

Egg Mayonnaise Dressing

There seems to be some myth behind mayonnaise making and some people swear that they can never get their mayonnaise to 'take'. It really is perfectly simple, particularly with the use of an electric blender or food processor. We have tried several ways of preparing a basic mayonnaise, and we find this one works best.

2 egg yolks, 2T cider vinegar or lemon juice, 1t mustard powder or fresh French mustard, 1t honey, pinch of pepper and vegetable bouillon powder, 10fl. oz or 300 ml of oil. (Olive oil makes a rather strong tasting mayon-

naise and we sometimes prefer to use a lighter oil such as cold-pressed walnut or soya.)

Put all the ingredients except the oil into the blender and process at top speed for about 45 seconds, then slowly trickle the oil in through the hole in the top of the blender in a thin continuous stream. This method really does work. One reason is probably that to make a successful mayonnaise you need your ingredients to be at room temperature, and by pre-blending you warm them all (especially if you are using refrigerated eggs).

This recipe makes about a cupful of mayonnaise. It should be refrigerated in an airtight jar to cool and then eaten within a day or two. (Bought mayonnaise only keeps so well because it is loaded with preservatives.)

Once you have your basic mayonnaise you can branch out with lots of interesting flavours and spices. Here are a few suggestions:

Green Mayonnaise Add a small handful of your favourite fresh herbs, finely chopped, or about a tablespoon of dried herbs such as parsley, oregano, thyme, dill, sorrel . . .

Garlic Mayonnaise Add a small crushed clove of garlic to the base.

Curry Mayonnaise Add a $^1/_2$t of curry powder and a dash of nutmeg.

Horseradish Mayonnaise Add 1t finely grated horseradish.

Hot Mayonnaise Add a dash of Tabasco sauce.

Tomato Mayonnaise Add 2T Whole Earth Tomato Ketchup.

Paprika Mayonnaise Add 1t paprika. 1t gives an attractive colour.

Mint Mayonnaise Add a handful of clean, de-stalked fresh mint leaves and blend.

Cheese and Onion Mayonnaise Add a little grated Parmesan or hard Cheddar and some very finely grated onion, chopped spring onions or chopped chives.

Tahini Mayonnaises

Basic Tahini Mayonnaise
¹/₂ C tahini, juice of 1 large lemon, ¹/₂ C water (or more)

Combine the tahini and lemon juice in the blender at medium speed. Add the water a little at a time to get the consistency you want.

You should keep the mayonnaise in an airtight jar and use it preferably the day you make it, but within 5 days at the most.

Plain tahini mayonnaise is a little bland on its own, but some delicious variations can be made.

Small Seed Tahini Mayonnaise Add either caraway *or* dill seeds, 1T cider vinegar, some finely grated lemon rind, a little honey and some finely grated onion if desired. You can sprinkle a few whole sesame or poppy seeds into the dressing just before you serve it.

Mexican Pepper Mayonnaise Add 2T finely chopped red and/or green sweet pepper, 1T finely minced onion, a pinch of cayenne pepper, a little mustard and ¹/₄t vegetable bouillon powder.

Herbal Mayonnaise Add $^1/_2 - 1$ clove garlic (crushed), fresh herbs if possible (chives, basil, chervil, parsley, lovage, rosemary, finely chopped), 1t vinegar and 1t honey.

Herbs

The magicians of Raw Energy food preparation, fresh herbs can transform a humble salad into a Pasha's delight. We use them constantly, lavishly, and occasionally with utter abandon – when we add as many as seven different leafy herbs to a simple green salad, becoming more of a herb salad than a green salad by the time we're finished. We never add salt to any of our dishes but when you rely on herb magic to garnish your salads, seed and nut cheeses, soups and hors d'oeuvres, even the most addicted salt user will find he hardly misses the stuff.

Most of our herbs we grow in the garden because there is something about freshness which you just can't recapture from the dried varieties. And with fresh herbs you needn't worry much about choosing the wrong ones. Some of our favourites for salads include lovage (which we also use to season many salad dressings), basil, dill, the mints, sweet cicely, winter savory, fennel, chives and the parsleys. In the summer we cull them from the garden. Some we dry by hanging from beams in our kitchen for a few days and then store them in airtight jars for winter use. Others – the more succulent herbs such as parsley, basil, and chives – can be deep frozen in sprigs then simply chopped and used when needed. If you live in a flat or don't have a garden you can grow herbs in pots in the kitchen window where they lend their own beauty to the room as well as offering a constant supply of culinary delights. Thyme, marjoram and winter savory will grow beautifully in pots indoors over the winter. So will parsley. Once you begin to play about with herb magic you will probably find, as we have, that you never want to be without these lovely plants.

Here are some of the most common herbs and what we find them useful for:

BASIL We probably use this herb far too much because it is available only in the summer months and because it is simply so lovely. It has a distinctive flavour which is an ideal garnish for tomatoes or in large amounts mixed into a green salad. Use the leaves whole for the best possible flavour.

CHERVIL This herb is a cousin to parsley, with a delicate aniseed flavour. We use it lavishly in salads. It mixes particularly well with chives, tarragon and parsley.

CHIVES More beautiful in looks than in flavour, we think, chives are great for sprinkling on to sunflower wafers or in seed cheeses. We find them not strong enough for most salads and prefer instead spring onions or a little chopped shallots.

DILL It goes wonderfully with yoghurt dressings, cucumbers, and beetroot and apple salads, and has a gentle delicate flavour which reminds one of quiet afternoons under sun-shaded willows.

FENNEL A lacy aniseed-flavoured herb which grows immense in the summer (ours is over eight feet tall). It goes well with salsify salads, and with cucumbers, tomatoes and in vegetables loaves. It is also a lovely decorative herb to place around the edge of dish salads.

HORSERADISH It is the root here which is important. Hot and pungent, it gets added to our many mayonnaises and dips for extra zest, and it works well in seed cheeses too.

LOVAGE Perhaps the most under-rated of the common herbs, lovage is wonderful mixed with the mints and yoghurt as the base of a herbal salad dressing which is as beautiful in colour as it is in flavour. We use lots of it also in our dish salads.

MARJORAM This herb comes in many variations – sweet marjoram, pot marjoram, winter marjoram, golden marjoram. Each is a little different. The sweet variety is lovely with plain green salads and goes well with tomatoes and Mediterranean vegetables. Oregano is a wild marjoram akin to our winter variety.

THE MINTS There are even more varieties than the marjorams – spearmint, peppermint, apple mint, pineapple mint, ginger mint, eau de cologne mint. We use spearmint and apple mint in green salads and many dressings. Pineapple mint with its splendid variegated leaves makes a wonderful garnish for fruit salads, drinks and also salad platters. Ginger mint is great (as are the others for that matter) in summer drinks, sorbets and punches.

PARSLEY This common herb comes in two main varieties – fine and broad leaf. For most raw dishes we prefer the broadleaf parsley because it is more delicate and pleasant to munch. Both have a rich 'green' flavour which works well with other herbs. It is great chopped in patties and loaves, in green salads and for dressings as well as being a lovely garnish for almost any dish.

SAGE This herb has a strong individual flavour and a particular affinity for onions. It is good in savoury nut dishes and adds flavour to seed and nut ferments.

SWEET CICELY Another aniseed-like herb which you can use as you would fennel. It is delicious in a carrot salad.

THYME It comes in many varieties, some of which are much richer in flavour than others, but all have a wonderful warming sweet flavour which enhances peppers, courgettes, and nut dishes as well as giving a unique flavour to sprout salads.

French Dressings

Oil dressings are especially good for leafy salads such as lettuce and spinach. With the right seasonings, such as a tasty mustard and various herbs, they can be very flavourful and not at all the 'plain oil and vinegar dressing' most people know.

Basic French Dressing
³/₄ C olive, soy or walnut oil, ¹/₄ C lemon juice or cider vinegar, 1t wholegrain mustard (French Meaux mus-

tard is our favourite) or mustard powder, 2t honey, a little vegetable bouillon powder and pepper to season, a small clove of crushed garlic (optional)

Combine all the ingredients in a blender or simply place in a screw-top jar and shake well to mix. Some people like to thin the dressing and make it a little lighter by adding a couple of tablespoons of water.

Here are some suggestions for dressings beginning with the French dressing base:

Rich French Dressing Add 1T tamari (see page 115), 1 finely chopped spring onion and a dash of cayenne.

Wine Dressing Add 1T of red or white wine – white is good for salads containing fruit, and red for cabbage salads.

Herb Dressing Our favourite combination of herbs for dressings is: marjoram, basil, thyme and dill or lovage (about 3–4T in all of fresh, finely chopped, or 2t dried).

Citrus Dressing Use $^3/_4$C sesame oil, juice of $^1/_2$ lemon and 1 orange, and 1T vinegar in the above basic dressing. Add 1t grated orange peel and $^1/_2$t grated lemon peel (scrub the fruits first!), a pinch of nutmeg and 1t chervil. Put all the ingredients in the blender until smooth.

Spicy Italian Dressing Follow the basic recipe, using cider vinegar, and add a dash of red wine or tamari, 2 ripe peeled tomatoes, 1T finely chopped onion, garlic, $^1/_2$t oregano and basil, and some powdered bay leaf. Blend all the ingredients well.

Olive Dressing Use olive oil and lemon juice in the basic recipe. Add 4–6 pitted black olives, finely chopped, and a pinch of cayenne.

Seed and Nut Dressings

Seed and nut dressings are particularly 'warming' served over a winter salad, and used over a sprout or mixed vegetable salad will make a substantial meal. There are two types – fermented and unfermented. Fermented dressings take about six to twelve hours to culture, depending on the temperature. They have a taste all their own which is both sweet and tangy. As with most dressings you can begin with the base and then add herbs and spices to suit your taste. Nuts and seeds can be fermented separately to make sauces, but we prefer them in combination.

Sunflower/Cashew Dressing
This dressing is good served over grated root vegetables such as carrots. You can ferment it or serve it immediately.

$^1/_2$ C cashews, $^1/_2$ C sunflower seeds, 1C water, 1t yeast extract or vegetable bouillon powder

Grind the nuts and seeds in a food processor as finely as possible. Add the water, then the yeast extract or vegetable bouillon and combine well. Put the mixture into a bowl and cover with a tea towel. Place in a warm spot for about eight hours (or overnight). After a couple of hours give the sauce a good stir. You may need to add more

water to make the dressing thinner. The ferment
should taste sweet and pleasant. If it tastes 'off'
you have over-fermented it. If you wish you can
season it lightly with a few fresh herbs before you
serve it.

Sun-Sesame Seeds Dressing

*$^1/_4$C sesame seeds, $^1/_2$C sunflower seeds (soaked over-
night in water), 1–2 carrots, juice of 1 lemon, 1t honey,
parsley, vegetable bouillon to taste, water*

Process the sesame seeds finely in the food processor, then add the sunflower seeds and re-process.
(The sesame seeds tend not to get ground up unless
they are done by themselves.) Add the roughly
chopped carrot(s), the lemon juice, honey and seasonings. Blend well. Add water to give the desired
consistency. You can use this one right away.

Italian Pesto

A delicious sauce, particularly good served over
alfalfa sprouts or a simple lettuce salad.

*Ideally use 1C of pine kernels (pignoli nuts) or pista-
chios (if you can't get these, or they are too expensive,
you can substitute almonds or pecans), $^1/_2$C olive oil,
1 handful of fresh basil leaves plus a little parsley or
oregano, $^1/_2$ clove crushed garlic, a little grated Parmesan or Sardo cheese (if desired)*

Blend or process the nuts and gradually add
the oil. Add the herbs (remove the stalks and use
only the leaves) and garlic, then add the cheese
and serve.

Sprouts

Seeds and grains are latent powerhouses of nutritional goodness and life energy. Add water to germinate them, let them grow for a few days in your kitchen and you will harvest delicious, inexpensive fresh foods of quite phenomenal health-enhancing value. The vitamin content of seeds increases dramatically when they germinate. The vitamin C can multiply five times within three days of germination – a mere tablespoon of soya bean sprouts contains half the recommended daily adult requirements of this vitamin. The vitamin B2 in an oat grain rises by 1,300 per cent almost as soon as the seed sprouts and by the time tiny leaves have formed it has risen by 2,000 per cent. Many sprouted seeds and grains also appear to have anti-cancer properties which is why they form an important part of the gentle natural methods of treating the disease.

When you sprout a seed, enzymes which have been dormant in it spring into action breaking down stored starch into simple natural sugars, splitting long-chain proteins into amino acids and converting saturated fats into free fatty acids. What this means is that the process of sprouting turns these seeds into foods which are very easily assimilated by your body when you eat them. Sprouts are, in effect, pre-digested and as such have many times the nutritional efficiency of the seeds from which they have grown. They also provide more nutrients ounce for ounce than any natural food known.

Another attractive thing about sprouts is their price. The basic seeds and grains are cheap and readily available in supermarkets and health-food stores – chickpeas, brown lentils, mung beans, wheat grains and so forth. And since you sprout them yourself with nothing but clean water, they become an easily accessible source of organically grown fresh vegetables, even for city dwellers. In an age when most vegetables and fruits are grown on artificially fertilised soils and treated with hormones, DDT, fungicides, insecticides, preservatives and all manner of other chemicals, home-grown-in-a-jar sprouts emerge as a pristine blessing – fresh, unpolluted and ready to eat in a minute by popping them into salads or sandwiches. As such they can be a wonderful health boon to any family concerned about the rising cost of food and the falling nutritional value in the average diet. Sprouts are the cheapest form of natural food around. Different sprouts mixed together will indeed support life all on their own. One researcher calculated that by eating sprouts alone you could live on less than 20 p per person per day. While we would certainly never suggest that anybody live on sprouts alone, we think they are an ideal addition to the table of every family – particularly if the budget is tight.

By the way, children love them since they can help grow them themselves. And because they grow so quickly – the average sprout is ready for the table in about three days – it satisfies their impatience. The youngest member of our family, when he was two, used to carry a little bag of sprouts around with him, munching them between meals as some children do sweets.

D-I-Y Sprouting

When you discover how economical and easy it is to grow sprouts, you will want to have some on the go all the time. Once germinated you can keep sprouts in polythene bags in the fridge for up to a week – just long enough to get a new batch ready for eating. Most people grow sprouts in glass jars covered with nylon mesh held in place with an elastic band around the neck, but we have discovered an even simpler method which allows you to grow many more and avoids the jar method problem of seeds rotting due to insufficient drainage.

You will need the following:

seeds (e.g. mung beans)
seed trays with drainage holes. These are avail-
    able from gardening shops and nurseries.
    (You can buy different sizes depending on
    the amount of sprouts you want to grow.)
a jar or bowl to soak seeds in overnight
a plant atomiser – available from gardening or
    hardware shops
a sieve
nylon mesh – available from gardening shops

1. Place two handfuls of seeds or beans in the bottom of a jar or bowl and cover with plenty of water. Leave to soak overnight.
2. Pour the seeds into a sieve and rinse well with water. Be sure to remove any dead or broken seeds or pieces of debris.

3. Line a seedling tray with nylon mesh (this helps the seeds drain better), and pour in the soaked seeds.

4. Place in a warm dark spot for fast growth.

5. Spray the seeds twice a day with fresh water in an atomiser and stir them gently with your hand in order to aerate them.

6. After about three days place the seeds in sun-light for several hours to develop the chlorophyll (green) in them.

7. Then rinse in a sieve, drain well and put in a polythene bag in the fridge to use in salads, wok-frys etc.

There are many different seeds you can sprout – each with its own particular flavour and texture. Use the chart below as a guide to the variety of sprouts you can try.

Sprouting Chart

SMALL SEEDS soak 6–8 hrs	Dry amount to yield 1¾ pints (1 litre)	Ready to eat in	Length of shoot (approx.)	Growing tips and notes
Alfalfa	3–4T	5–6 days	1½ in (3.5 cm)	Rich in organic vitamins and minerals, the roots of the mature plant penetrate the earth to a depth of 30–100ft (10–30m).
Fenugreek	½C	3–4 days	½ in (1 cm)	Have quite a strong 'curry' taste. Best mixed with other sprouts. Good for ridding the body of toxins.

Mustard no soaking needed	1/4C	4–5 days	1 in (2.5 cm)	Can be grown on damp paper towels for at least a week; the green tops are then cut off with scissors and used in salads.

LARGER SEEDS soak 10–15 hrs	To yield 3 1/2 pints (2 litres)	Ready to eat in	Length of shoot (approx.)	Growing tips and notes
Adzuki beans	1 1/2C	3–5 days	1–1 1/2 in (2.5–3.5 cm)	Have a nutty 'legume' flavour. Especially good for the kidneys.
Chickpeas	2C	3–4 days	1 in (2.5 cm)	May need to soak for about 18 hours to swell to their full size. The water should be renewed twice during this time.
Lentils	1C	3–5 days	1/4–1in (0.5–2.5 cm)	Try all different kinds of lentils – red, Chinese, green, brown. They are good eaten young or up to about 6 days old.
Mung beans	1C	3–5 days	1/2–2 1/2 in (1–5 cm)	Soak at least 15 hours. Keep in the dark for a sweet sprout. Put a weight (plastic bag filled with water and tied) on the beans to get long straight sprouts.
Soya beans	1C	3–5 days	1 1/2 in (3.5 cm)	Need to soak for up to 24 hours with frequent changes of water to prevent fermentation. Remove any damaged beans which fail to germinate.

Sunflower	4C	1–2 days	Same length as seed	Can be grown for their greens. When using sunflower seeds soak them and sprout for just a day. They bruise easily so handle with care.

GRAINS soak 12–15 hrs	To yield 1³/₄ pints (1 litre)	Ready to eat in	Length of shoot (approx.)	Growing tips and notes
Wheat	2C	2–3 days	Same length as grain	An excellent source of the B vitamins. The soak water can be drunk straight, or added to soups and vegetable juices.
Rye	2C	2–3 days	ditto	Has a delicious distinctive flavour. Good for the glandular system.
Barley	2C	2–3 days	ditto	As with most sprouts, barley becomes quite sweet when germinated. Particularly good for people who are weak or underweight.
Oats soak 5–8 hrs only	2C	3–4 days	ditto	You need whole oats or 'oat groats'. Oats lose much of their mucus-forming activity when sprouted.

Raw Power for Slimming

So useful is a Raw Energy way of eating for slimmers that the vast majority of people find when they begin eating this way they shed any excess weight slowly and naturally without ever having to count calories or restrict the quantities of energy rich foods such as seeds, grains and oils.

To anybody who has conscientiously fought (and frequently lost) the battle of the bulge, this can seem almost a miracle. It is not. It is simply a physiological result of the kind of re-balancing which takes place in the body on a high-raw diet. In our experience about 80 per cent of Raw Energy slimmers fall into this category. The other 20 per cent (to which, incidentally one of us belongs – Leslie) are only slightly less fortunate. For us to lose weight we have simply to cut back on the fattier foods such as the seed and nut cheeses and to avoid the richest of the salad dressings while eating as much as we like of the rest.

Slimming Secrets

Using the Raw Energy way of slimming works in several ways. First, it supplies your body with the highest complement of nutritional support it can get anywhere in the form of vitamins, minerals, easily assimilated proteins, and essential fatty acids so that you don't suffer the fatigue often linked with a calorie-restricted diet; neither do you end up with those dangerous sub-clinical vitamin deficiencies associated with off-again-on-again crash regimes. Second, the natural fresh foods we use in our recipes are rich in fibre. This is particularly important to slimmers since a high-fibre way of eating not only makes you feel full and satisfied – provided you are eating the right kind of soluble fibre (bran is *not* this kind, incidentally) – but it will also help your body stabilise blood-sugar levels and thereby reduce feelings of hunger. Some kinds of fibre such as pectin, which is found in good quantities in apples and some other fruits, help detoxify your body of poisonous wastes such as heavy metals like lead and aluminium.

Raw Energy eating centred around large quantities of fresh raw vegetables also offers enormous help to slimmers, thanks to the high potassium content of these foods and to their ability to make the body more alkaline. The by-products of the average Western diet rich in meat, sugar, coffee and processed foods, are highly acidic. Like stress, they tend to make the blood more acid. Taken over a long period of time such foods can put considerable strain on your body's natural mechanisms for maintaining its proper acid/alkaline balance.

Slimming itself tends to render your blood more acidic because the by-products of fat burning also tend to be acid. This can make slimmers feel nervous and irritable. The high potassium content of fresh raw vegetables and some fruits, and the ability these foods have to alkalinise the body, helps eliminate that unpleasant feeling of strain and nervousness slimmers know so well, and leaves you feeling well and calm as the pounds melt away.

An End to Cravings

Raw Energy slimming also works for many for whom no other slimming method has been successful, because it helps wipe out the cravings for foods that seem impossible to resist and which defeat many slimmers. You know the kind of thing: you go to the cupboard and reach for a biscuit to go with your tea and you find yourself eating the whole packet. This results in feeling desperately guilty, in the sense that you feel hopeless, with 'no will power'. It also results in your trying to cut back on what you eat during the rest of the day to make up for all those extra calories. For many would-be slimmers this leads eventually to nutritional deficiencies and chronic fatigue which only make matters worse.

Such cravings – and the kind of uncontrollable eating which they spur – are often the result of a food intolerance, sometimes called a food allergy. As experts in food allergies will tell you – for complex biochemical reasons – you will tend to crave those foods to which you are intolerant or allergic, so that they become a kind of addiction. You simply can't stop eating them once you take a bite or two. This is a common problem – particularly among those who have experienced the off-again-on-again slimming.

The most frequently occurring intolerances centre on milk and milk products and wheat. They are foods which we therefore tend to eliminate from the menus of those people who are intent upon losing weight, but are not as fortunate as the 80 per cent who lose it naturally on a 75 per cent raw diet. They need extra help, and eliminating milk and wheat products brings this help to many. You will find the recipes in this section therefore contain no milk, cheese or yoghurt products, and no wheat flour or anything containing it. If you are one of the would-be slimmers who knows this craving pattern only too well you are likely to find that steering clear of these things will make all the difference in the world.

The Principles of Slimming

Simple. Here they are:

*Eat three meals a day.
*Make sure at least 50–75 per cent of what you eat is raw.

*Stress the energy-light-but-fibre-rich foods in your diet – particularly fresh raw vegetables, grains and pulses.

*Drink only *between* meals but then as much as you like.

*Chew your foods long and carefully.

*Indulge yourself in the splendour of many different dishes chosen not only from this section but others as well (leaving out milk and wheat products if you are not losing weight fast enough to please you).

*Enjoy your foods. Delight in them. Enjoy too the 'automatic will power' that seems to come when your body slowly re-balances itself through Raw Energy eating.

The Slimmer's Day

A sample menu would be as below:

SLIMMER'S PORRIDGE
PACKED LUNCH – CRUDITÉS,
SPROUTS, DIP AND FRESH FRUIT
SLIMMER'S DINNER – PORTUGUESE
PRAWNS with HOT SPICY SAUCE,
BROWN RICE, GREEN SALAD AND
FRESH FRUIT

The slimmer's choice of recipes in this book is almost as broad as any other's. Except for the rich dressings, cheeses and desserts which contain a lot of nuts and oils, the Raw Energy recipes are naturally ideal for slimming. The number of crunchy raw vegetables you can fill up on is unlimited. Be sure you dress them with one of our lighter dip-dressings such as Tofu, Raw Hummus or Curried Avocado and you'll be on the way to a slimmer you in no time.

Breakfast is very much like the Raw Energy muesli except that it includes the three seeds. These supply the essential fatty acids which everyone – even slimmers – need. Too many would-be skinnies avoid 'fat' in every form and end up with peeling skin and dull hair, as well as more serious deficiency problems. By including the right amount of good fats in your diet you will help avoid that feeling of your body 'needing' something while steadily shedding excess pounds. The oats and fruit in the porridge are an excellent source of fibre. You will find that the breakfast leaves you full and satisfied so that you are less troubled by hunger pangs and more able to stick to your regime.

Lunch is a packed lunch which includes lots of crudités, some sprouted beans, a tofu dip and a piece of fruit. For most people, especially those who go to work or school, lunch is the worst time of all for snacking on fattening foods. If you simply pack a box chock-a-block with good munchy foods you can reach for them at lunch-time (or snacktime) to satisfy your pangs.

Dinner is based around a large salad with a bowl of rice (or any other grain such as millet or buckwheat) and a little meat, fish, game or pulses etc. plus a little fresh fruit for dessert. The meal can consist of Green Salad with Spicy Tomato dressing which doubles up as a cocktail sauce for the Portuguese Prawns, a bowl of brown rice topped with chopped spring onions, and a bowl of black grapes.

Breakfast
Slimmer's Porridge

2T oatflakes (soaked overnight in water), 1 pear or apple (grated), 1 finely chopped banana, juice of 2 oranges, 1T minced three-seed mix (pumpkin, sunflower, sesame), pinch of cinnamon

Combine the soaked oats with the fruit and orange juice and mix well. Sprinkle with minced 3 seeds and dust with cinnamon. Enjoy!

As a variation try replacing the banana with other fruit such as a peach or a handful of strawberries. Or blend in a food processor to make a smooth porridge.

Lunch
Fill a lunch box with the following:

Crudités
These vegetables and fruits make ideal crudités: carrot sticks, celery sticks, broccoli and cauliflower florets, rings or strips of red, yellow and green peppers, mangetout, diagonal slices of cucumber, courgette, thin slices of Jerusalem artichokes, white radish and kohlrabi, whole radishes, button mushrooms, spring onions, celery hearts, tomatoes, red and white cabbage slivers, apple wedges, orange segments, watercress, pineapple, olives.

A container of Tofu Dip (see page 34).
A small plastic container of mixed sprouts – e.g. mung, lentil and chickpea.
An apple or other piece of fruit.

Dinner

Prepare a Green Salad.
Arrange several cooked prawns over the salad.
Prepare the following sauce:

Spicy Hot Sauce/Dressing
This makes enough to use several times – store in a screw-top jar in the fridge.

6 ripe tomatoes, handful basil leaves, 1t Meaux mustard, 1 egg yolk, 2t vegetable bouillon powder, few drops Tabasco, juice of 1/2 lemon, 1t honey, 1T tomato purée, 1T minced onions, 1 crushed clove garlic

Process the tomatoes very finely. Add the other ingredients and blend well.

Bowl of hot brown rice.
Bowl of black grapes.
A glass of spring water with a twist of lemon if desired.

This is just one example of a slimming 75 per cent raw way of eating. There are plenty of other recipes – for salads, soups, dressings and desserts which a slimmer can feast on without feeling guilty or putting on weight.

Tea 'n' Treats

The worst health offenders in most ways of eating – particularly children's diets – are processed sweets made from refined sugar. Not only are they bad for teeth, they can cause more serious problems in children such as sub-clinical deficiencies or hyperactivity, and in adults can contribute to the development of degenerative diseases such as diabetes, arthritis and coronary heart disease. However, trying to get children to give them up is like pulling teeth from a hippopotamus. Far better to give them a wholesome alternative to replace those chocolate bars, biscuits and cakes.

In this section you will find recipes for all sorts of sweet treats, each made from nutritious ingredients – nuts, seeds, dried fruit, coconut, carob and honey – which can be served at tea time with one of our delicious shakes or smoothies, or taken to school in a lunch box to snack on. They are as tasty as they are wholesome.

Sweet Treats

These attractive little sweets can be wrapped in coloured paper and given in boxes as gifts for Easter, Christmas etc.

1C mixture of almonds and hazelnuts, 1C mixed dried fruit (such as date and apricot, peach and raisin, or sultana and pear), 1T honey, juice of 1 orange or ½C apple juice, dash of orange liqueur (optional), coconut flakes and sesame seeds

Put the nuts and the dried fruit in the food processor and chop thoroughly. Add the honey and enough fruit juice to make the mixture bind, plus a dash of orange liqueur if desired. Remove from the processor and roll into spheres the size of large marbles. Sprinkle a plate with the coconut flakes (toasted if desired) and sesame seeds and roll the balls in either one or both. Chill in the fridge and serve on a platter decorated with fresh fruit.

Carob and Apple Cake

This is a wonderful Raw Energy cuisine replacement for Black Forest Gâteau!

1C sunflower seeds (or a 2:1 mixture of sunflower and sesame seeds), 1C carob powder, ½C dried coconut, ½C dried pitted dates, 3 apples, ½t vanilla essence, 1t allspice, apple slices or strawberries to garnish

Grind the seeds very finely. Add the carob powder, coconut and dates. Quarter and core the apples, then homogenise in the food processor with the dry ingredients. Add the vanilla essence and allspice. Spoon the mixture into a flat dish and leave to chill for a couple of hours in the fridge. Decorate with apple and/or strawberry slices before serving.

Shortcake Biscuits

These are great served as wafers with fresh fruit salad.

1C oatflakes, ¹/₂ C dried dates, ¹/₃ C dried coconut, 1–2t vanilla essence, 1T honey

Process all the ingredients together well. Remove the mixture and squeeze off a small portion in your fist to make an oval shape. Press this flat on to a board, then turn it with a fish slice and flatten it on the other side. Place the wafers on a plate and chill in the fridge for at least half an hour.

Rocky Road Bananas

This is a great recipe if you have too many ripe bananas on your hands. Once frozen the bananas will keep for weeks – unless they are eaten immediately as in our house!

4 ripe bananas, ¹/₂ –1C coarsely ground Brazil nuts, honey

Simply peel the bananas and skewer on to kebab or ice lolly sticks. Roll in honey and then in chopped nuts. Put on a freezer-proof plate and freeze until hard. Eat straight from the stick. If you prefer you can first slice the bananas cross-wise, coat in honey and sprinkle with nuts, then freeze to make bite-sized treats.

As a variation try mixing a few tablespoons of carob powder into the honey to make chocolate coated bananas and then roll them in coconut, dates or nuts . . . or all three!

Porcupine Pineapple Chunks
A lovely idea for children's parties.

Cut a fresh pineapple into cubes and skewer on to cocktail sticks. Roll in clear honey and then coat with wheatgerm, sesame seeds or coconut. Chill and serve.

Yoghurt Lollies
The best ice-lollies are home-made. You can buy ice-lolly moulds and sticks in most department stores. We mix a large bowl of plain yoghurt with some frozen concentrated orange juice, then pour the mixture into the lolly moulds and freeze. You can also add fresh fruit and honey to natural yoghurt and blend it together to use, or simply freeze fresh fruit juices such as orange, grape, apple and pineapple.

Sorbets
The easiest way to make sorbets is with a sorbe-tière – a special machine which stirs the sorbet or ice cream as it freezes it. We have survived for many years without one by improvising . . .

Orange Sorbet Juice 8 oranges and then combine in the processor with 2 juicy seedless oranges which have been peeled and quartered. Add enough honey to sweeten and some nutmeg or ginger if desired. We sometimes like to add a grated peach or two to give the sorbet texture. Pour the mixture into ice-cube trays or a plastic lunch-box type container and freeze. Remove from the freezer and leave for about ten minutes to thaw slightly. Blend the mixture again immediately before serving and spoon into glass dishes or into empty halved orange shells.

Strawberry or Blackberry Sorbet Combine 3C berries with 2 bananas and a little honey. Follow the method as above. The bananas give a creamy texture to the sorbet.

Carob and Honey Ice Cream

This recipe is one of our family favourites. The combination of carob and honey we find unbeatable.

2 pints (about a litre) milk (we use goat's but you can use cow's or even skimmed milk if you like), 2 egg yolks, 3T granular lecithin (optional but very nice since it gives a creamier texture), 1C unheated carob powder, $^1/_2$C clear honey, 1t pure vanilla essence

Freeze the milk in a low flat plastic container. When frozen, remove from the freezer and let sit for about half an hour until it is just soft enough to slice into pieces. Put the egg yolks into the food processor, add about a cup of the frozen milk, the lecithin, carob powder, honey and vanilla, and blend thoroughly using the blade attachment. Add the rest of the frozen milk and continue to blend until it is just mixed. (Don't overblend or you will make the ice cream too liquid.) Should it become too liquid simply re-

turn to the freezer for a few minutes then stir
before serving. Serve immediately.

Drinks

Cherry Whip (for 1)
*1C natural yoghurt, ¹/₂ C pitted black cherries, 2t honey,
double cream (optional)*

Blend the yoghurt, cherries and honey and
pour into a tall glass. Top with a spoonful of
double cream and garnish with a pair of cherries
hung over the edge of the glass. As a variation use
strawberries or raspberries instead of cherries.

Banana Shake (for 1)
Peel and freeze a ripe banana, then chop it into
fairly small pieces and blend with a cup of milk
and a dash of vanilla essence. Sweeten with honey
if desired.

Mocca Milk (for 1)
*1C milk, ¹/₃ C carob powder, 1t instant cereal 'coffee'
(chicory or ground barley based), 1T honey, vanilla
essence, whipped cream and chopped pecans to top*

Mix a little of the milk and the carob into a paste
and put it in the blender with the rest of the milk,
the 'coffee', the vanilla essence and the honey.
Blend well and pour into a glass. Top with a little
whipped cream and chopped pecans if desired.

Golden Smoothie (for 2)
*2 oranges, 2 peaches, 1 banana, 1t orange bitters or
1t vanilla essence, 1t nutmeg, a little honey if desired*

Peel the oranges and remove the pips. Homogenise in the food processor with the peaches and banana. Add the orange bitters or vanilla, the honey and the nutmeg. Combine well. Pour into two tall glasses with crushed ice and serve.

Garden Punch (for 4)

This is our favourite summer drink. To make a large jugful, you will need:

A large handful of fresh mint and lemon balm, 2C water, a handful of raspberries or blackcurrants, 1 orange, 1 lemon, 2C apple or grape juice, 1C pineapple or orange juice, 1C fresh elderflowers (de-stalked), honey, ice

Blend the fresh mint and lemon balm with the water and berries until the leaves are finely chopped. Add the grated rinds of the orange and lemon and leave the mixture to soak in the blender for at least fifteen minutes (preferably longer). Pour the other juices (apple or grape and pineapple or orange) into a jug. Squeeze the lemon and slice the orange. Add to the jug, then add the elderflower heads (these can be strained off later, but a few poured into the glasses with the drink are particularly attractive). Strain the mint mixture into the jug and discard the leaves, berry pulp and rinds. Sweeten with a little honey and chill. Serve in tall glasses with ice and fresh mint. You can also add a few other flowers from the garden such as orange blossom or lilac.

Herb Teas

Our rich and delicious shakes and drinks are not for everybody. Kids love them but adults often prefer a simple tisane or herb tea which is light and refreshing, and can be drunk either hot with a little honey for sweetening, or made double strength, chilled and served in a tall iced glass. Herb teas make seductive and healthy alternatives to tea and coffee.

They come in two varieties – those which you take for medicinal purposes such as red sage as a gargle for a sore throat, dandelion to eliminate excess water from the body, lemon grass for indigestion and St John's Wort for skin problems – and those which you drink for pure pleasure. Some such as camomile and vervain (which are natural sedatives) and peppermint (which calms the digestive system) belong in both. Our favourites include lemon grass, lemon verbena, orange blossom, hibiscus and lime blossom.

You can either make your own from dried herbs or you can buy herb teas ready packaged in bags which you use as you would ordinary tea bags – allowing them a little longer to steep. There are some wonderful herbal combinations on the market in these little bags – cinnamon and rose flavour, for instance, or apple and cinnamon. Or you can drink each tea separately.

Home-made Herb Teas
It takes about a tablespoon of the dried herbs (either a single herb or a mixture) to make two

cups. Pour boiling water over it and let it steep in a pot for five to ten minutes, stirring every now and then to extract the full aroma. Now strain and serve with a slice of lemon and/or a little honey for sweetening. Sometimes we add cinnamon to herb teas and even a teaspoon of fresh cream.

In the summer drink them iced. We keep a teapot full of our favourite tea in the fridge drinking it often instead of eating snacks. But make it double strength and make sure if you want sweetening that you dissolve the honey in your tea before you chill it. Serve it with a twist of lemon in a tall glass with a sprig of mint or a pair of cherries sitting on the edge. Sometimes we even freeze small flowers such as honeysuckle, lilac or elderflower into cubes of ice and float these in the tea. Herbal flowers such as hibiscus give a beautiful red colour to chilled tea served in a tall glass.

Raw Juices

Fresh pressed apple, grape or carrot juice is like nectar from the gods compared to the bottled variety you can buy. And raw juices have remarkable healing properties. They form the base of what we think is the best contribution the Germans ever made to renewing vitality and good looks. It's called the Rohsäfte-Kur. Europeans use it to revitalise themselves after a long winter when people eat too much, exercise too little and spend far too many hours in heated offices and houses. We use it when we are feeling 'dead' from too much stress, too little sleep or just simple fatigue. The Rohsäfte-Kur is simply a raw juice regime which you carry out over a day or even a few days to spring-clean your system and make you feel super-alive – mentally clear and beautifully receptive to things around you. It makes your skin glow and also quickly trims away a few excess pounds.

Raw juices are exceptionally rich in health-producing enzymes as well as vitamins, minerals and trace elements useful in restoring biochemical balance to the body. According to authorities on the Rohsäfte-Kur, raw vegetable and fruit juices accelerate the burning up and elimination of accumulated wastes. This is why a day or two on juices is the cornerstone of rejuvenation treatment at many expensive European health resorts.

Raw juices cannot be made in a food processor or blender. They require a special juice extractor – usually a centrifuge affair into which you feed the fruits and vegetables as it chops them and spins out their precious juices. Then you are left with the juice which you drink and the pulp which you toss into the compost. The health-promoting properties of fresh juices depends on their being drunk live – that is within a few minutes of being made – so that the oxidation process which sets in almost immediately does not destroy essential vitamins and enzymes. We find, however, that if you make a thermos full of juice and chill it immediately by filling it with ice cubes it will keep for several hours so you can take it to work or drink it throughout the day when you feel thirsty.

But raw juices are by no means only valuable because of their therapeutic properties. Some – such as fresh apple, grape and pineapple – are also the best tasting drinks we've ever come across. We often use raw juices to make delicious chilled soups as well, and, mixed together with mineral water, herbs and flowers, to make dazzling summer drinks.

If you are the fortunate owner of a juice extractor you should take the time to experiment a little to see which juices you prefer and what works best for you. We often make a base of carrot and apple – about half and half – to which we add smaller quantities of other juices such as cabbage, beetroot, berry, etc. Here are a few of the most common juices and some of their uses:

CARROT An excellent juice for alkalinising the system and therefore for countering stress. It is rich in carotene which the body turns into vitamin A – an important nutrient in protecting you from infection and early ageing. It also contains vitamins C, D, E and K. Useful for rebuilding healthy tissue and for treating skin problems.

APPLE Also a great cleanser, apple juice is believed to purify the blood and is useful as a general tonic. It contains vitamin C, many of the B complex vitamins, and lots of potassium and folic acid. Apple juice also helps overcome any sort of digestive upset.

CUCUMBER This juice is a natural diuretic – it encourages your body to get rid of excess water stored in the tissues. Drunk regularly it can be an aid to healthy hair and nails, thanks to its high sulphur and silicon content. We prefer cucumber juice mixed with, say, apple or carrot or both, since its taste is slightly insipid.

CABBAGE Not a nice tasting juice – cabbage needs to be mixed with carrot or something else as well – but it is also an effective internal cleanser and has been used medically as a treatment for healing stomach ulcers. Not useful for anyone with a sluggish thyroid, however, since cabbage can suppress thyroid activity somewhat.

GRAPE This juice is famous not only for its deliciousness but also for its natural sugars which are traditionally considered ideal for a short spring-clean regime. Warning: once you have tasted real fresh grape juice you will never again be content with the bottled variety!

Fabulous Feasts

The *Shorter Oxford English Dictionary* defines feast as 'A sumptuous meal or entertainment for many guests . . . something delicious to feed on.' We might add – a spread of food which not only tastes splendid, but is also seductive to the eye – a real hedonist's paradise. That is how we feel about what we call our Fabulous Feasts.

We delight in preparing numerous delicious Raw Energy dishes for our large family and many friends. We love to try out bounteous combinations of different tastes, colours and textures with the least possible excuse for celebration. It's challenging, it's fun, and it is always different. In this chapter we hope to give you some hint of just how splendid Raw Energy cuisine can be for parties and celebrations and to give you some of our favourite recipes for hors d'oeuvres, raw soups, main courses, side dishes and sweets. We hope you will like them as much as we do.

Hors d'Oeuvres

Mushroom Flower Cups

8–12 large button mushrooms, ¼ C almonds (ground), 3T yoghurt, a squeeze of lemon juice, 1t honey, 1t dill seeds (roasted and ground), fresh parsley, vegetable bouillon powder, fresh mint

Remove the stalks of the mushrooms. Grind the almonds as finely as possible and mix with the yoghurt, lemon juice and honey. Add the ground dill seeds, a little chopped parsley and some bouillon powder. Spoon this mixture into the mushroom cups. Serve in twos or threes on little dishes garnished with mint sprigs.

Green Crêpes

These are stuffed lettuce leaves. The leaves need to be large and flexible so that they roll without splitting. For the stuffing we use finely chopped vegetables in a creamy egg or tahini mayonnaise (see page 54). A combination we particularly like is:

alfalfa sprouts, avocado, tomato, red pepper, spring onions, finely grated carrot or beetroot

Finely chop or grate the vegetables and mix them together with the dressing of your choice. Put spoonfuls of the mixture on to the lettuce leaves, roll them up and spear with a cocktail stick to hold in place.

Salad Kebabs

Skewered rows of different vegetable and fruit chunks make a very unusual and appetising starter. Make Salad Kebabs by skewering different things on wooden kebab sticks, such as:

button mushrooms, pitted olives, cherry tomatoes, pepper chunks, cucumber chunks, diced tofu or cheese, soaked dried prunes or apricots

Serve your skewers with a spicy dressing on a bed of shredded lettuce.

Soups

Carrot Chowder

This is one of our raw soups which can be warmed to just above blood heat (not over 40°C as this will kill the enzymes and some of the vitamins), or serve chilled.

³/₄C walnuts/pecans, 8 carrots, juice of 3 oranges, 2C water, 1 egg yolk, 2t vegetable bouillon powder, dash of white wine, ¹/₂t fresh grated nutmeg, a few chopped chives to garnish

Grind the nuts in a food processor. Add the carrots, roughly chopped, and re-process. Finally add the orange juice, water, egg yolk, bouillon, wine and nutmeg. Combine thoroughly. Serve at once or warm gently for a minute or two. Pour into individual bowls and top with chopped chives.

Gazpacho

This soup is particularly delicious served with 'croûtons' – roasted soya nuts or wheat and barley roasts (see page 51).

1T minced onion, 3 tomatoes, 1 red pepper, 2 small cucumbers, 3 egg yolks, 3T vinegar, 3T olive oil, 1 clove garlic, 1/2 C tomato juice, 2t vegetable bouillon powder, 1t honey, dash of red wine (optional), 2 spring onions, fresh parsley and basil

Purée the onion, tomatoes, half the red pepper and one of the cucumbers in the blender or processor, then add the egg yolks, vinegar, olive oil, garlic, tomato juice, seasoning, honey and wine. Finely chop the spring onions, the other cucumber and the remaining red pepper and fresh herbs and add to the soup when you serve. Put the croûtons in a separate dish for people to help themselves.

Fresh Green Soup
2 avocados, 2C apple juice, 1–2C water (depending on how thick a soup you want), 2 lemons, 1t vegetable bouillon powder, parsley, lovage, dash of white wine, the centre stalks of a head of celery

Peel and stone the avocados and process with the apple juice, water, 1 heaped teaspoon of chopped lemon rind, the juice of the lemons, bouillon, parsley, lovage and wine. Chop the celery stalks, including the leaves, and add to the soup. Blend well and serve garnished with a thin slice of lemon.

Main Courses

The main course of our Fabulous Feasts is usually one of our Supersalads (see pages 39–67), perhaps with some rice, buckwheat, millet or a baked potato on the side. Sometimes we prepare a Sunburst Platter of crudités instead of a salad, and serve it with one of our vegetable loaves.

Sandstone Loaf

This dish has a beautiful pink/orange colour.

6 carrots, 3 sticks celery, juice of 1/2 lemon, 1/4 C almonds, 1/4 C pumpkin seeds, 2T tahini, 1/2 onion, a handful of fresh parsley (or 1T dried), 2t vegetable bouillon powder, 1T grated beetroot

Wash the carrots and celery. If the celery is stringy, peel away the tougher fibres with a knife. Roughly chop the carrots and celery and put into the food processor. Homogenise thoroughly, adding the lemon juice, and put into a separate bowl. Now grind the nuts and pumpkin seeds well. Add them to the carrot and celery mixture and stir in the tahini, finely chopped onion, parsley, bouillon and grated beetroot. Pack into a bread tin. Garnish with parsley leaves and almonds and serve from the tin.

Fermented Seed Loaf

This loaf is best fermented for several hours, so make it ahead of time.

1/2 C almonds, 1/2 C sesame seeds, 2T tamari, 1 clove garlic, basil, parsley, 1t caraway seeds, 1/2 –1C water, 1C chopped cauliflower or broccoli florets, 4 mushrooms, 2 sticks celery, radish slices to garnish

Finely grind the nuts and seeds. Add the seasonings – tamari, chopped garlic, basil, parsley, caraway seeds – and the water. Finely grate the cauliflower or broccoli and dice the celery and mushrooms. Mix all the ingredients together and pack into a bread tin. Cover with a tea towel and leave to ferment for several hours in a warm place. Add radish slices just before serving.

Desserts

Our desserts vary from the very simple, such as slices of fresh fruit sprinkled with ginger, to the more elaborate – our Stuffed Pineapple Salad or Raspberry Freeze Pie. Either way they are the crowning delight of a splendid feast and leave you feeling light and energised rather than bloated and drowsy.

Stuffed Pineapple
1 large pineapple, 1 orange, 1 mango or papaya (chopped), 1C raspberries or strawberries, 2 figs (fresh, or dried ones, soaked), dried coconut to garnish (optional)

Slice the pineapple in half lengthwise and remove the flesh from each half, leaving a $^1/_2$ inch (1 cm) shell. Dice the flesh and mix it with the sliced orange, mango (papaya) and raspberries (halved strawberries). Finely chop the figs and add. Mix all the ingredients together and spoon into the pineapple shells. Sprinkle with dried coconut and serve.

Raspberry Fruit Freeze Pie
There are many variations that can be made on this theme – using different berries and fruit to fill the raw pie base.

Pie Base
1C pitted dried dates, ¹/₂ C almonds, ¹/₂ C oatflakes, 1t honey, a little water

Grind the dates and almonds as finely as possible in a food processor. Add the oats, honey and a little water and blend again. You need to add the water slowly to get the right consistency. You want the mixture to bind but not be sticky. Remove the base from the processor in a ball and flatten it into a pie dish with your fingers. As a variation you can add a tablespoon or two of coconut.

Pie Filling
2 bananas, 2C raspberries, sherry, honey to sweeten

Peel the bananas and chop into pieces about an inch (2.5cm) or so thick. Freeze in a polythene bag with the raspberries until firm. Remove from freezer and blend the fruits together with a dash of sherry and a little honey to sweeten if desired. Pour into the pie crust and serve immediately garnished with a few banana slices or raspberries.

Strawberries and Cashew Cream
One of our favourite ways of eating strawberries is to pick them and leave their stalks on, then wash them well and serve with a bowl of yoghurt or sour cream and another of honey or raw sugar. Those with a sensitivity to milk can still enjoy strawberries and cream by making their own non-dairy 'cream' from cashew nuts, and pouring it over a bowl of ripe fresh strawberries.

Cashew Cream

1C nuts, ¹/₂ C water or orange juice, 1–2t honey, nutmeg

Blend the nuts and liquid as finely as possible in the blender or processor. Add a little honey and nutmeg and use as a topping for any fruit.

Cooking Foods

We recommend a diet of about 50 to 75 per cent raw food, so what about the other 25 per cent? Well, first you'll notice how cooked ingredients tend to creep into our raw recipes and salads: toasted sesame seeds or almonds for salad sprinkles; toasted coconut for sweet coatings; or roasted spices, such as dill, in dressings. Toasting nuts, seeds and spices brings out the subtle flavours of their aromatic oils and affords a greater range of tastes. For the rest we never allow cooked foods to become the focus of a meal, but rather enjoy them as 'side dishes'. And when we do cook something we pay great attention to *how* in order to preserve as much of its nutritional value as possible.

For instance, we would never dream of boiling a vegetable. Too many vitamins are destroyed in the process and too many minerals lost in the water as it is discarded. Vegetables are good steamed when you cook them. You can buy a

Packed lunch – crudités with tofu dip, sprouts and fresh
fruit

(*Above*) Wok-fried vegetables

(*Left*) Garden Punch

(*Overleaf*) The raw elements of a fabulous feast

steamer or improvise one using a colander placed in a saucepan to which you add a small amount of water. Even better – both for flavour and nutrition – are stir-fried vegetables done instantly in a wok so they remain crisp in the minutest quantity of olive or soy oil – oil which is never heated to the smoking point.

If we cook game or fish we cook it as slowly as possible to ensure it retains its natural juices and flavours. If you are a meat eater there is a lot to be said for game and fish. Unlike the meat from our domestic animals – beef, lamb, pork, etc. – both game and fish are low-fat foods. And of the fats they do contain, most are unsaturated. Also, because these creatures are not intensively farmed they do not contain the worrying array of chemicals our domestic animals now do.

Most of the foods we serve cooked, however, are not the meats and fishes, but rather what we call the 'peasant foods': soups, grains, pulses and porridges, Scottish oatcakes and dark German rye breads. We love thick country soups to go with our fresh salads and seed cheeses, particularly in winter. Many of these soups are based on the pulses – peas, beans, lentils – or the grains such as millet, oats, barley or brown rice. These foods are wonderfully rich in fibre and offer low-calorie, low-fat, sustaining energy. And peasant foods are not expensive either. Neither are potatoes – one of the most underrated of all the natural foods. We bake ours in their jackets and eat them whole filled with home-made dips sprinkled with chives. New potatoes we steam gently without peeling and serve with chopped fresh mint and a little butter.

Change Slowly

One of the most important things to remember when adding more fresh raw foods to your diet is that it is best done slowly, slowly. This is for two reasons. First, changing your diet dramatically in any direction can cause digestive upset simply because the human body tends to rebel against whatever it is not accustomed to. Second – and more important – changes made slowly are far more likely to last.

Begin by making one meal a day a huge salad. Then notice how much better you feel in a week or two. As you look better, feel better and begin to discover for yourself the high energy potential such a way of eating offers, you will find yourself automatically including more and more fresh foods in your menu. This way the process of change becomes a natural evolutionary one from which not only you will benefit. Others will, too, as they notice how much Raw Energy is doing for you and become curious to follow your example.

Meanwhile enjoy your steak if you want it, or your cream buns. Neither of us would ever re-strain ourselves from eating a piece of chocolate cake if we felt we wanted it. It is just that when you have tried enough pieces of chocolate cake and you remember what it feels like to eat such foods, you find after a while you don't want them any more. Fresh strawberries dredged in coconut seem more appealing.

Here are some of the cooked foods we often eat and some of our favourite family recipes. We hope you like them.

The Beautiful Grains

Brown rice, wheat, barley, oats, millet, bulgar wheat and buckwheat are wonderful staple foods – high in fibre, a good source of protein when eaten with vegetables, and very filling. They are exceptionally good for athletes, slimmers and people who want to have sustained energy. The basic rule for cooking grains is you need about $1/2$ a cup of dry whole grains to serve each person.

The first thing to do with your grain is to wash it in cool water, using a strainer, to gently loosen the dust and small bits of dirt. Check to see there are no little bits of rock left. When the water through the strainer rinses clean they are ready to cook.

There are two basic ways of cooking whole or cracked grains. The first uses cold water mixed with the grain. The second adds boiling water to the grain. We prefer the boiling water method.

Sauté the grain either in a heavy dry pan or with the smallest amount of olive oil possible to brown it a little. (This is not necessary with rice or barley, but the others benefit greatly from it.) Now add boiling water, a handful of herbs and some vegetable bouillon powder to the pot and cover immediately. Bring to the boil and continue to cook at a simmer on the hob or (we prefer this) pop it all into a moderate oven to finish. (Do not stir the grains as this breaks them up and makes them stick in clumps.)

Every grain needs a slightly different length of cooking time. Here are some guidelines.

BROWN RICE

Use twice as much water as rice and cook for 45 minutes. Usually we cook rice by simply adding cold water to the grain, bringing to the boil and then simmering.

MILLET AND BUCKWHEAT GROATS

One part grain to two parts water for 20–25 minutes. Millet can be cooked by the cold water method.

BULGAR WHEAT

This is wheat which has been cracked, toasted and steamed before you buy it. Use one part bulgar wheat to one and a half parts water. Cook for 20 minutes.

BARLEY

Use twice as much water as grain and cook for 1 1/2 hours.

How do you serve grains? There are so many delicious ways: on their own with some herbs tossed in; with a few vegetables such as onions and mushrooms; cold leftover grains mixed into salads; and in thick nourishing country soups.

The Humble Pulses

One cup of beans, lentils or peas measured dry makes about four average servings. Like the grains, these inexpensive foods are also rich in fibre and have good sustaining power. And they come in such wonderful varieties – black beans, limas, kidney, soya, lentils of all sorts and colours, adzuki beans and chickpeas. These too we mix with salads sometimes. We also use them as the base for delicious soups and we casserole dishes with them lavished with fresh herbs.

Here's how to cook the pulses. We usually soak our pulses for several hours – or overnight in a cool place – before cooking them. This softens them and cuts the cooking time considerably. It also helps break down some of the starches they contain and renders them more digestible. After soaking throw the soak water away, put them in a pot, add three times as much water as pulses, bring to a boil and simmer until done. These too can be cooked in the oven instead of on top of the hob. We prefer oven cooking because you don't have to be so accurate about the time you take them out and because they are less likely to stick to the pot. Beans and lentils love carrots, onions and celery which we often add as well as herbs and seasoning. (Our famous vegetable bouillon powder works its magic here as well.)

Here's a brief guide to timings:

RED LENTILS
Twenty minutes (don't need soaking either).
SPLIT PEAS AND OTHER LENTILS
One hour.
OTHERS (EXCEPT SOYA BEANS)
One and a half hours.

SOYA BEANS
Two and a half hours.
CHICKPEAS
One and a half hours.

Soups

Our winter soups are hearty and full-bodied. We make them from whatever vegetables we happen to have, adding some millet, lentils, peas, rice, barley or whatever is handy for thickening, lots of fresh herbs from the garden or a few dried herbs, and perhaps some bouillon powder for seasoning. Here are three examples.

Thick Vegetable Soup
This makes enough for a good four to six servings.

4 carrots, 2 turnips, 2 leeks, 1 head celery, 1 parsnip, 2C garden peas, 1C runner beans, plus any other vegetables you happen to have (or substitutions), 2T olive oil, 1T vegetable bouillon powder, 2 bay leaves, 3 pints (1.5 litres) stock or water, 3/4 C brown rice or millet, fresh parsley

Wash and peel the vegetables. Cut root vegetables into small cubes, the leeks first lengthwise four to six times then across so you get tiny pieces. Add oil to pot and sauté leeks. Then add chopped celery, carrots, and turnips, putting the lid on to allow them to sweat for five minutes. Now add the vegetable bouillon, bay leaves, stock or water (boiling) and the rice, and allow to cook for 30 minutes. Now add peas and beans and cook for another 15 minutes. Sprinkle with chopped parsley and serve.

Borscht

This serves four to six people well.

3 raw beetroot (with their tops if possible), 1 medium onion, 3 carrots, 1/2 small cabbage, 2T olive oil, 2 pints (about a litre) stock or water, 1T vegetable bouillon powder, juice of 1 lemon, 3T honey, 1 cup of thick yoghurt or sour cream, a dash of nutmeg

Wash vegetables – do not peel – and cut them into small strips. Retain half of one beetroot which you will add grated to the soup later. Heat oil in pot and sweat beetroot and onion for five minutes, then add the rest of the vegetables, including the sliced beet greens, and stew for another five to ten minutes, stirring occasionally. Add boiling stock or water – together with bouillon powder, and cook vegetables until tender. Now add lemon juice, grated beetroot and honey and cook for another five minutes, then serve topped with the thick yoghurt or sour cream and grated nutmeg.

Potato Soup

This, too, serves four to six people.

6 medium potatoes, 2 1/2 pints (scant 1.5 litres) water or stock, 1t vegetable bouillon powder, 1C sliced, chunked or diced vegetables (such as leeks, celery, carrot, swede, green beans, peas, etc.), herbs (such as marjoram, winter savory, basil and garlic), garnishes (such as sliced spring onions, chopped hard-boiled egg, chives, watercress, or grated hard cheese)

Scrub potatoes and wash vegetables, cutting them into medium-sized chunks. Cover the potatoes with the water or stock to which the bouillon has been added and boil until tender. Remove from heat and blend in a food processor until smooth. Now sauté the vegetables (cut into small pieces) and add them to the potato mixture along with herbs, and cook for five minutes. Sprinkle with your garnishes and serve.

Wok Frying

The most delicious way of all to cook vegetables is à la Chinoise – in a wok or frying pan. It is quick, simple and a lot of fun to do. Here's how.

Use no more than 2T soy or olive oil, then take whatever vegetables you happen to have. A good combination is:

a handful of cashews, cauliflower (broken into florets), mangetout (topped and tailed), onions (cut in rings), red pepper (diced), mushrooms (sliced), spring onions (spiked – their green parts slit lengthwise), tamari

Put the oil into your pan and heat. Add cashews on their own and brown, then add vegetables which take longest to cook such as onions and cauliflower. Sauté for two to three minutes, turning constantly. Now add the rest of the vegetables and continue to toss them in the pan for another three to five minutes. Add a little tamari and serve.

A Guide to Raw Energy
Shopping

Not only are the methods of food preparation
and the equipment you need different in preparing Raw Energy foods, so is the shopping. You will
find your larder stocked with a whole new set of
ingredients – particularly if until now you have
been living on the average Western fare of fast
foods or meat and two veg. The delicious foods
which you will use for most of these recipes are
not only good for you, most of them are very tasty
on their own – grains and legumes, nuts and
seeds, fruits, vegetables and herbs.

These foods can either be bought at great cost,
or, if you shop around, very cheaply. Because we
have a large family we buy many of our fruits in
crates from a wholesaler at less than half the
price you pay in your greengrocer. You can pay
dearly for nuts and seeds, grains and pulses in
some health-food stores where they come in tiny
packages (and are often not very fresh either).
But pulses can be bought cheaply in the average

106

supermarket and nuts, grains and dried fruit can be purchased at reasonable cost from many of the new whole-food emporiums which are appearing around the country. Obviously the more you buy at one time the cheaper they are. Be sure to refrigerate your nuts after purchase to keep their oils from going rancid. And if ever you buy a package of anything which you find on returning home is not absolutely fresh, take it back and complain. That is the only way to protect yourself while improving the quality of what is being sold.

Here is a brief guide to stocking a Raw Energy larder to give you some idea of just how much variety you have to choose from.

First of all the fresh fruits and vegetables which *must* be refrigerated.

Fruits

Fruits are often divided into different groups depending on which combine best together for digestion.

'ACID'
Orange, lemon, grapefruit, lime, strawberries, pineapple, pomegranate, plums (and prunes), blackberries, raspberries, black and red currants, tangerine, kumquats, ugli.

'SUB-ACID'
Apple, apricot, figs, grapes, mango, papaya, pear, peach, cherries, blueberries, nectarine, kiwi, lychees, passion fruit.

'SWEET'
Banana, dates, persimmon, most dried fruit.

'MELONS'
Watermelon, cantaloup, honeydew, cassaba.

Fresh Vegetables

There are basically three categories: leaves, roots
and fruit vegetables:
LEAVES
Lettuce (Cos, Chinese, iceberg, Webb's Wonder,
lamb's or corn salad, romaine, red or radicchio,
Boston), cabbage (red, white, green), cress
(watercress, land cress, mustard and cress), spinach, endive (curled, round-leaved, French), chicory, beet tops, dandelion leaves, kale, Brussels
sprouts, ruccola.
ROOTS
Carrot, beet, radish (horseradish, white radish),
turnip, parsnip, celeriac, Jerusalem artichoke,
kohlrabi, salsify, fennel.
FRUIT VEGETABLES
Cauliflower, avocado, broccoli, onions (leeks,
spring onions, red onions, shallots), celery, peppers (red, green, yellow), tomatoes, cucumbers
(courgettes, auber-gine, young marrows, squash),
peas and beans (legumes), mushrooms (fungus).

Cereals

These figure in many of our mueslis and savoury
recipes. Those we use most often are: wheat, rye,
oats, barley and millet. These can be bought in
'flake' or cut form and soaked to use in mueslis,
or bought whole and sprouted for salads.

Millet is a particularly good grain and worth getting to know. It is the only alkaline grain and the only grain that contains all eight essential amino acids. It can be used sprouted, or cooked.

Buckwheat, often classified as a grain, is in fact a member of the Polygonacea family which includes rhubarb and sorrel. It is the triangular seeds of this plant that are sold. They are often pre-roasted, but can be bought raw. As with millet they can be eaten cooked or sprouted.

Oils

Buying good oil is very important. The best kind is fresh unrefined, cold-pressed extra virgin olive oil. This is because it is a monounsaturated oil and as such much more stable than the polyunsaturates from corn, peanuts, sunflower or safflower seeds. It is also extracted from the fruit by mechanical pressing rather than by heat and chemical processing methods. As such the fatty acids it contains are in a form that your body can make good use of for building cell walls, making hormones and keeping nerve sheaths strong and healthy. In heat-processed oils, such as most you find on supermarket shelves, these usable 'cis' fatty acids have been chemically changed into 'trans' fatty acids which can not only be actively harmful, they can actually block the uptake of any essential 'cis' fatty acids in the rest of your diet as well.

Olive oil is good and adds a distinctive flavour to salad dressings. It is quite heavy, though, and some people prefer a lighter oil. Soya oil and walnut oil are lighter, and both are delicious too. Walnut oil is wonderful (but it's expensive).

Nuts

When buying nuts make sure they are really fresh. The rancid oils in old nuts are harmful to the stomach, retard pancreatic enzymes, and destroy vitamins. If nuts are fresh and whole (unbroken) you can buy a kilo or so at a time and, provided they are kept airtight in a cool dry place (best in your refrigerator), they will keep for a few months. You can even freeze them. It is a good idea to buy a few different kinds. Then if you mix them you will get a good balance of essential amino acids. You will also have more variety in your recipes.

Choose from: almonds, Brazils, cashews, coconut (fresh or desiccated), hazels, macadamia nuts, peanuts (strictly speaking a legume), pecans (similar to walnuts, but less bitter), pine kernels, pistachios, tiger nuts and walnuts.

Seeds

Again be sure you buy really fresh seeds with no signs of decay. The three seeds which provide such a valuable combination of protein and essential fatty acids are sunflower, pumpkin and sesame. Other seeds worth trying, mainly for seasoning, are poppy, celery, caraway, dill, fennel and anise. The last four make good snacking 'sweets', separate or in combination. In the eighteenth and nineteenth centuries people used to carry a mixture of these seeds in their pockets whenever they went out to meetings and would munch on them to keep their appetites at bay.

Legumes and Other Sprouts

Remember, all whole seeds, grains and sprouts are living things and should be stored and handled with care.

Here are a few kinds of sprouts (for more ideas see page 65): alfalfa seeds, adzuki beans, mung beans, lentils, fenugreek, radish, chickpeas, soya beans and peas.

Special Foods

CAROB (ST JOHN'S BREAD) Carob powder/flour is a superb chocolate substitute – and good for you too. Unlike chocolate it does not contain caffeine. Instead it is full of minerals – calcium, phosphorus, iron, potassium, magnesium and silicon – as well as vitamins B1, B2, niacin and a little vitamin A plus some protein. Carob powder is often sold toasted, but the best kind is raw. It is lighter in colour than the cooked kind. It can be bought from most health-food stores and used to make chocolate drinks, desserts and treats.

TOFU This is soya bean curd made from soya milk. All soya bean products are very high in protein and low in carbohydrate so they make a good food for dieters. Soya beans also contain a high amount of lecithin which fights the build-up of cholesterol deposits and is needed for the proper functioning of the brain and nervous system. Soya is a highly alkaline food. Both soya milk and tofu can be found in health-food stores. They don't have a strong flavour, but taste slightly nutty and are quite palatable. One disadvantage to soya products is that, unless they are cooked or made from the sprouted beans, they contain phytic acid which binds the important mineral zinc and prevents its absorption.

WHEATGERM A delicious and valuable food high in vitamins E and B complex. Like molasses, it is the 'goodness' that is removed from the original product (in this case wheat) when it is refined. It should be bought raw, vacuum packed, not 'toasted', and then refrigerated to keep it fresh and can be used liberally sprinkled on salads, mueslis, desserts and so forth.

COCONUT Besides fresh coconut you can buy natural coconut in two forms – flaked or shredded. Make sure the kind you buy has not been sweetened with sugar or glucose syrup as so many are. For most uses we prefer the shredded. We sprinkle it on mueslis and use it a lot in treats. It keeps well for weeks in the refrigerator.

DRIED FRUIT When buying these be sure they are not dipped in glucose (figs and banana chips as well as pineapple, mango and papaya usually are). Also, try to find sun- rather than sulphur-dried fruit: raisins, sultanas, currants, apricots (look out for the unsulphured, unpitted Hunza ones), peaches, prunes, pears, figs, dates and bananas.

Sweeteners

HONEY This makes a wonderful substitute for sugar in drinks and desserts. There are so many sorts ranging from very mild – such as acacia or orange blossom – to very strong, such as Mexican honey or Tupolo from pines. If you don't like one kind, don't be put off, there are plenty of others to try. Clear honeys are best for drinks whereas set honeys, such as clover, are nice on breads. The best honeys are those labelled 'organic' as many commercial ones are made using sugar-fed bees. Honey contains many useful trace minerals.

MOLASSES This is one of the 'super-foods'. It is the leftover bulk from sugar refinement and is as good as bleached sugar is bad. It contains all the minerals and vitamins that are taken out of processed sugar. It is particularly rich in B complex vitamins and minerals. Much molasses is quite overpowering in its flavour and tends to have an unpleasant sulphur tang. This is because sulphur has been used in the sugar-extraction process. Unsulphured molasses, however, is quite delicious and can be eaten straight off the spoon. If kept in the refrigerator it becomes firm and thick and is wonderful on muesli or in yoghurt and spread on bread.

The best kind of sugar is raw cane or molasses sugar as it is unrefined. Billington's Golden Granulated sugar is the best. But with honey and molasses, you really don't need to use sugar and you're better off without it. Also, when you eliminate sweet foods from your diet you find that you really don't want them any more.

Herbs and Spices

Remember to buy spices in small quantities from shops with a good turnover, as they soon lose their freshness. The most flavourful herbs are freeze-dried, but these are hard to find. Vacuum-sealed herbs are a good bet. Remember to store your herbs and spices in the dark as the light affects their potency (so much for herb and spice racks!). For the sake of flavour it is best to buy whole spices and grind them yourself when needed in a coffee grinder or with a pestle and mortar. If you've never ground your own you'll be amazed at the splendid aroma and taste. With fresh herbs, wash and dry them well, then store in sealed polythene bags in the salad compartment of your fridge.

The list that follows contains many seasonings that you will find in the recipes.

'SWEET' SPICES (for fruit salads and dressings, desserts and ethnic dishes)

Allspice, angelica, aniseed, cardamom, cinnamon, cloves, coriander, ginger, nutmeg and mace.

'SAVOURY' SEASONINGS (for salads, soups and raw main dishes)

Basil, bay, caraway seeds, cayenne pepper, celery seeds, chervil, chilli powder, chives, coriander leaves (fresh), cumin, curry powder, dill, fennel, garlic, horseradish, juniper berries, kelp, lemon balm, lovage, marjoram, mint, mustard seeds, onion, oregano, paprika, parsley, pepper, poppy seeds, rosemary, sage, savory, sorrel, tarragon, thyme.

SAVOURY SEASONING POWDER This seasoning is useful for those times of panic when you
just don't know what to add to give your dish the
'something' that it needs. Our rescue remedy
that we wouldn't be without is a wonderful vegetable bouillon powder made by Marigold Health
Foods Limited, Unit 10, St Pancras Commercial
Centre, 63 Pratt Street, London NW1 OBY. Tel:
071 267 7368, and called simply *Swiss Bouillon
Powder*. Buy the low-salt variety. It has more flavour. We use it in dressings, sauces, ferments,
soups, seed and nut dishes–just about every-
where.

Condiments and Other Flavourings

Some other useful additions for the larder shelf:
MUSTARD Mustard can be bought in dry or
paste form. The dry powder is sometimes useful
in dressings. We think the most delicious mus-
tards are French. They are milder and more aromatic than English mustard. Moutarde de Meaux
is particularly delicious and is great in dressings
for all sorts of salads. Dijon and Bordeaux are
also nice.
TAHINI (preferably unroasted). This is made
simply from finely ground sesame seeds and has
many uses including tahini mayonnaises, as an
addition to many seed and nut dishes, and mixed
with honey as a topping for fruit and desserts.
TAMARI This is a type of soya sauce made from
fermented soya beans, but unlike soya sauce it
contains no wheat. Unfortunately it does contain

sea salt, so it should be used in moderation. Nevertheless, it is good for giving a 'Chinese' taste to dishes as well as a rich flavour to bland dressings or sauces.

YEAST EXTRACT This can be used as a substitute for 'vegetable bouillon'. It is rich in B complex vitamins, but very salty, so it should also be used in moderation.

VINEGAR Apple cider vinegar is the best as it contains malic acid which is helpful in the digestive process.

VANILLA ESSENCE Try to find real vanilla essence rather than the more common vanilla flavouring which is synthetic. Used in nut milks or yoghurt drinks and desserts, it gives a delicious warm flavour.

Raw Food Cautions

Some foods should not be eaten raw. Pulses and beans, for instance, have a number of negative attributes. Soya beans, broad beans and kidney beans contain a trypsin inhibitor. This substance blocks the action of certain enzymes in the body so that not all of the essential amino acids the beans contain can be used. Many years ago researchers discovered that soya beans would not support life unless they were cooked for several hours. In the human body the trypsin inhibitor is believed significantly to alter the nutritional value of proteins, rendering them virtually useless for us. When these foods are cooked or sprouted, however, the trypsin inhibitor is eliminated and they are rendered good to eat.

Chickpeas and green peas also contain a trypsin inhibitor but one which is not neutralised by heat, and peas contain a haemaglutin which resists heat. Haemaglutins inhibit growth in an animal by combining with the cells in the lining of the intestine and blocking nutrient absorption. But the trypsin inhibitor in chickpeas is rendered harmless when they are sprouted and the harmful elements in peas occur in such small quantities that many people eat them both raw and cooked without any adverse effects. Eating raw lima beans or red kidney beans, however, has been known to cause death.

The Brassicas

Cabbage, Chinese cabbage, watercress, kale, swede, turnip, rape, Brussels sprouts and mustard belong to a genus called Brassica. They contain compounds called thioglucosides which disrupt the functions of the thyroid gland and have been shown to contribute to the development of goitre. Similarly, drinking the milk of animals who have been grazing on these plants can interfere with thyroid function. But the negative effect of the Brassicas is eliminated provided you have adequate iodine in your diet. It is something we never worry about for it is only people deficient in iodine who suffer them.

The Raw Egg

People are also often cautioned against eating raw eggs. Provided they are free-range and salmonella-tested, raw egg yolks are fine but the white of an egg contains avidin, a substance which combines with biotin and prevents it from reaching the blood. This could lead to a biotin deficiency. In a young man who ate many raw egg whites on their own symptoms such as scaly skin, anaemia, anorexia, nausea and muscle pains developed. The albumen in the egg white also dissolves in water and can easily enter the blood-stream undigested resulting in allergies. This is, of course, only in extreme cases and is far more likely if someone is eating the raw egg whites on their own rather than in combination with the yolks.

We generally prefer to use only the raw yolk in our recipes. However we do not think twice about preparing a delicious egg nog occasionally. It is simply a question of moderation.

Sprouting Improves Safety and Quality

Because of the massive enzyme release which oc-curs when a seed or grain is sprouted the nutri-tional quality of a sprout is extremely good as well as its 'safety'. These enzymes not only neutralise such factors as trypsin inhibitors but also destroy other substances which can be harmful such as phytic acid. Phytic acid, which occurs in consider-able quantity in grains, particularly wheat, tends to bind minerals so that the digestive system can-not break them down for assimilation. When a grain is sprouted this mineral-binding capacity is virtually eliminated.

Did You Know That . . .

Athletes Can Improve Their Performance on Raw Foods

Professor Karl Eimer, director of the First Medical Clinic at the University of Vienna, put top athletes into a high-intensity training programme for a fortnight and then suddenly changed their diet to one of entirely raw foods. His athletes grew stronger, faster and more supple.

Raw Foods are a Boon to Slimmers

The uncooked fibre which they contain decreases the amount of fat absorbed during digestion, creates a feeling of fullness and satisfaction, and spring-cleans the body of waste products that can make you feel tired. Raw foods also decrease food sensitivity reactions which lead many people to over-eat from cravings, raise energy levels and, thanks to their alkalinising quality, enhance your ability to deal with stress.

The High-Raw Diet Benefits the Whole Person

It offers the perfect and complementary combination of all the nutrients essential for maximum vitality, both of the body as a whole and on a cellular level. Raw foods increase the micro-electrical potentials of cells, improving your body's use of oxygen so that both muscles and brain are energised.

Raw Foods are Perfect Spring-Cleaners of the Body

They help you eliminate stored wastes and toxins which interfere with the proper functioning of cells and organs and lower your energy levels.

Raw Foods are Central to the Gentle Approach to Treating Cancer

A typical anti-cancer regime, used effectively for almost 100 years in Europe, consists of organically grown foods and juices made from them. On this regime 80–90 per cent of foods are eaten raw.

Our Bodies React to Cooked Foods as an Invasion

Research done at the Institute of Clinical Chemistry in Lausanne showed that the body recognises cooked and processed foods as invaders. They trigger the body's defence system – sending white blood cells into the intestine as soon as the food enters the mouth. Eating raw foods leaves your white blood cells free for other tasks and saves the body the effort of a defensive action, thereby strengthening its resistance to disease.

Diabetics and Arthritics Have Been Cured on Raw Food Diets

The tradition of treating degenerative diseases on a high-raw diet is a long one. At some of Europe's most famous clinics, such a diet is still used to lower blood pressure and cholesterol levels and treat many other major and minor problems.

Index

123

INDEX